HE NEVER TURNED ANYONE AWAY

THE HOSPITALITY OF JESUS CHRIST

Lee Shipp

xulon PRESS

He Never Turned Anyone Away
The Hospitality of Jesus Christ
by Lee Shipp

Printed in the United States of America

ISBN 9781607919209

www.xulonpress.com

OTHER BOOKS BY PASTOR LEE SHIPP

God is Not Dead and Neither Am I
Available through First New Testament Church).

Why Live This Way ... When You Don't Have To?
Breaking Strongholds
(Available through Xulon Press, Barnes and Noble, Amazon.com,
And First New Testament Church.)

Even Now ...
The Resurrection of Your Hopes and Dreams
(Available through Xulon Press, Barnes and Noble, Amazon.com,
and First New Testament Church.)

DEDICATION PAGE

To the Eternal King, who in the perfect display of hospitality, died for us all.

Upon Whom the Spirit rested, anointing Him to:

Heal our broken hearts,

Deliver us from bondage,

Restore our sight,

And remove our oppressions –

To convince us that God accepts us poor, helpless sinners through the gospel He came to preach.

ACKNOWLEDGEMENTS

I wish to acknowledge the Body of Christ! The Lord has graciously allowed me to minister to His Body in so many places around the world. Every culture is unique with its own beauties and differences, but one thing remains unchanging in every part of this planet, in the Church of Jesus Christ there is the family of God. Through the indwelling Christ, His kind love and benevolent Spirit comes through His people without fail. So let me thank all of you true believers who have shown me the Hospitality of our beautiful Lord Jesus.

I must also thank Janice McCoy for her diligence to take my inept ability to write and transform it into something that is worth reading. Thank you for the sacrifice you have made to make my thoughts and words flow with grammatical sense.

TABLE OF CONTENTS

JOHN 13: 1-17

Now before the feast of the Passover, when Jesus knew that his hour was come that he should depart out of this world unto the Father, having loved his own which were in the world, he loved them unto the end. And supper being ended, the devil having now put into the heart of Judas Iscariot, Simon's *son*, to betray him; Jesus knowing that the Father had given all things into his hands, and that he was come from God, and went to God; He riseth from supper, and laid aside his garments; and took a towel, and girded himself.

After that he poureth water into a basin, and began to wash the disciples' feet, and to wipe *them* with the towel wherewith he was girded. Then cometh he to Simon Peter: and Peter saith unto him, Lord, dost thou wash my feet? Jesus answered and said unto him, What I do thou knowest not now; but thou shalt know hereafter. Peter saith unto him, Thou shalt never wash my feet. Jesus answered him, If I wash thee not, thou hast no part with me. Simon Peter saith unto him, Lord, not my feet only, but also *my* hands and *my* head. Jesus saith to him, He that is washed needeth not save to wash *his* feet, but is clean every whit: and ye are clean, but not all. For he knew who should betray him; therefore said he, Ye are not all clean.

So after he had washed their feet, and had taken his garments, and was set down again, he said unto them, Know ye what I have done to you? Ye call me Master and Lord: and ye say well; for *so* I am. If I then, *your* Lord and Master, have washed your feet; ye also ought to wash one another's feet. For I have given you an example, that ye should do as I have done to you. Verily, verily, I say unto you, The servant is not greater than his lord; neither he that is sent greater than he that sent him. If ye know these things, happy are ye if ye do them.

INTRODUCTION

THE TEST OF TRUE FAITH

Why a book on hospitality? Search your local bookstore, even perform an internet search and see how little has been done on the subject. However, hospitality characterized the most significant aspects of Jesus' ministry. Many may confuse hospitality with service, but the difference is noteworthy.

The Random House Dictionary defines hospitality as the friendly reception and treatment of guests or strangers ... the quality or disposition of receiving and treating guests and strangers in a warm, friendly, generous way. Jesus described these guests and strangers this way. On one occasion Jesus was asked, "Who is my neighbor?" And Jesus said,

A certain man went down from Jerusalem to Jericho, and fell among thieves, which stripped him of his raiment, and wounded him, and departed, leaving him half dead. And by chance there came down a certain priest that way: and when he saw him, he passed by on the other side. And likewise a Levite, when he was at the place, came and looked on him, and passed by on the other side. But a certain Samaritan, as he journeyed, came where he was: and when he saw him, he had compassion on him, And went to him, and bound up his wounds, pouring in oil and wine, and set him on his own beast, and brought him to an inn, and took care of him. And on the morrow when he departed, he took out two pence, and gave them to the host, and said unto him, Take care of him; and whatsoever thou spendest more, when I come again, I will repay thee. Which now of these three, thinkest thou, was neighbour unto him that fell among the thieves? And he said, He that shewed mercy on him. Then said Jesus unto him, Go, and do thou likewise (Luke 10:29-37).

You see many can serve without heart and affection, but you cannot be hospitable without sincere heart and affection. You can serve and not really let others into your life, but you cannot be hospitable and keep people at a distance. Hospitality is the act of bringing people in for the purpose of caring, being kind, and showing them generosity. To be hospitable is to deliver men from their sickness, to care for them until they are well. It is more than easing the pain, it is to rescue them from their peril and lead them to life in all its fullness!

The world is broken. Humans are suffering. Families are dealing with runaway children, teenage pregnancy, divorce, suicide, drug addiction, internet pornography and this list goes on. Most people cannot take it anymore. They are scared, wounded, and defeated, fettered in chains they cannot escape – yet you hold the key! You are the means by which God wants to demonstrate His love!

Michael Green, in his book, *Called to Serve*, says,

When we reflect on the history of the Church, are we not bound to confess that she has failed to follow the example of her Founder? All too often she has worn the robes of the ruler, not the apron of the servant.

Why should you invest your time with this book on Hospitality? Because it is written for you, that you may be encouraged to throw your life into the most significant endeavor upon this planet! That you may be the catalyst which forever changes the destiny of men. I want you to know that God is looking for you, calling you unto His fields. He desires your partnership. And what is your benefit? Exploding joy, contentment, eternal rewards, and a walk with Jesus!

God did not choose great men and women who were grown up in ministry or trained for ministry to impact society. Instead He chose carpenters, fishermen, tax collectors, and shepherds. These were people who worked hard. People who worked days, nights, and overtime – these were the men that Jesus chose! He did not choose the Pharisees, Sadducees, and scribes- those who were refined in religious culture. Even so today, He chooses those who know how to work hard. If people do not work hard in the secular world they are not going to work hard in the ministry!

God does not want you in a place where everybody serves you, but rather where it becomes your joy and delight to serve other people. This is the humble heart. This is the godly heart. This is the life that God can speak through and use. What is important in the kingdom of heaven and most beneficial to God's eternal plan is that we are going to serve God and man.

The role Jesus assumed that last night with His disciples (washing the disciples' feet) was the role of the lowest servant among the slaves. Jesus, knowing the contention among His disciples had to provide a drastic illustration of humility. He moves and takes a towel, a basin of water, and the dirty feet of His disciples. He then illustrates the most important lessons of His kingdom: Don't be selfish; love God and man more than you do yourself. And do not think more highly of yourself than you should.

The true test of our service is not that we do these things but the nature in which we do them. You see, Jesus was showing us the secret of joy. He was saying that when we do things like this it is then that we are acting most like Him. But the most important thing is the nature of how we serve. Many will serve religiously and perform their actions with a false piety and others will serve grudgingly.

Paul said it is possible to give all your possessions to the poor and your body to be burned and it profit you nothing. I would hate to consider that you lived a life of hospitality only to discover in the end that it was to no avail! You see, the purpose of this book is not simply to give you nice things to do. The motive and objective of your hospitality matters! You can be busy doing nice things, and yet your heart may be wrong. I do not want your labor in Christ to be in vain.

Jesus shows us the most significant things in life are not the big things we consider to be "spiritual" but the common things. True spirituality is taking advantage of the common things God gives us to do every day – that is the mind-set of the spiritual person.

You may think the spiritual person is the one who walks into the pulpit of your church on Sundays. But there might be nothing spiritual about that person. The spiritual person is not necessarily the one who goes on the mission trips. Many people can get psyched up for such a trip.

The most spiritual may be the person that is seldom in the spotlight. He never preaches, he never teaches; yet everyday he lives before God. Every day he goes to his job. He punches in on time. He works really hard as unto the Lord. He is admired and has favor with man. He is adorning the gospel of God with such beauty that people want to know the hope that he has in the Lord. He is faithful and diligent. He has lived before God in prayers and fastings. He demonstrates Christ in all his behaviors - that is the spiritual person! Our opportunities of hospitality are set before us every day, it is not when we walk on water but when we see the basins of water behind the door, and we take the towel and serve somebody!

Most Christians will live their entire lives having never raised the dead. Most will never walk on water. Most will never speak to a large crowd of people. Most will never see thousands of people come to Christ as a result of their preaching ministry. But if you do what God has called you to do, even if it is in the secular field, you will be rewarded well.

Anybody can do the things that please God: Feeding the hungry, clothing the naked, ministering to the needy, and preaching the gospel to the poor. What an impact. You don't need the elaborate.

By human measurements, religion has set standards regarding spiritual status and significance which most people sitting in our congregations will never attain. One of those measurements is that a Man of God must be in full-time ministry, such as a pastor or evangelist. Such a standard is disastrous and discouraging because most believers will never be called to an office in the Body of Christ.

Because of these standards many in Christ will be overlooked for their value among God's people. Their valuable contributions and spirit-anointed life will not be appreciated, and a valuable work of God, which could come through them, is neglected.

It is my desire to encourage the lay person in Christ, that the life he lives can be used for eternal purposes even though he is not called to a specific office. I long for the layman to be excited about going to his job everyday knowing that it is his mission field, and he is reaping eternal rewards for Jesus Christ.

I want you to realize that the opportunity to show hospitality is at the heart of the gospel of Jesus Christ. In the synagogue, Jesus announced His intentions and the prophetic ministry entrusted to Him,

> The Spirit of the Lord *is* upon me, because he hath anointed me to preach the gospel to the poor; he hath sent me to heal the brokenhearted, to preach deliverance to the captives, and recovering of sight to the blind, to set at liberty them that are bruised, To preach the acceptable year of the Lord. And he closed the book, and he gave *it* again to the minister, and sat down. And the eyes of all them that were in the synagogue were fastened on him. And he began to say unto them, This day is this scripture fulfilled in your ears (Luke 4:18 – 21).

When Jesus came to the world he reached out to those who were sick, to those who were cast out, and to the unaccepted. He preached the acceptable year of the Lord. Those that were bruised, He came to deliver. For those held captive, He came to set them free. Jesus expressed His gospel through hospitality. He laid down his life every day to relieve the distressed. And in like manner, we are able to validate our faith by laying down our lives for one another: in our churches, in our homes and families, and for the strangers we may meet.

Distributing to the necessity of saints; given to hospitality (Romans 12:13).

CHAPTER 1

TOWELS, DISHES, AND SANDALS
WHAT GOD VALUES MOST

—

For none of us liveth to himself, and no man dieth to himself.

- The Apostle Paul

S pirituality has to do with conduct and character not vocation!
For thirty years the son of God worked in the carpentry shop
of Joseph. Jesus worked in that shop as unto His Father and God the
Father took that as spiritual and worshipful. He was diligent. He was
not lazy … slothful … irresponsible. Any passerby, while observing
Jesus in the carpentry shop, would never consider His work to be
of a spiritual nature. To so many shallow minds spiritual things are
only demonstrated in healing the sick, walking on water, raising the
dead, preaching in the synagogue; those individuals who think on
such a shallow level can never understand how making a chair can
be spiritual. But in the way Jesus thought, lived, and acted; everything He did was spiritual in its nature. That is His character!

When we talk about spirituality we are not talking about a particular vocation, some religious act or deed. Many people may "do"
what others call spiritual (preaching, inner city work, teaching …).
However, those who are accomplishing these "spiritual feats" may
not be spiritual in the least bit. Spirituality has to do with character;
it has to do with the nature of a person not just his actions!

Consider this example. When the Bible says that we are to pray
in the name of Jesus, it simply means that we pray in submission to
His will. We are in Christ and representing Christ; therefore, we are
asking the things He would ask. Our desires are His desires. If we
were asking selfishly for our own interests alone, then we would be
praying in our own name; though we conclude our prayers with, "In
Jesus name, Amen." Simply ending all prayers with, "… in Jesus
name, Amen." does not constitute praying in Jesus' name. This is not
the magical phrase that gets the answer. Instead, to pray in "Jesus

name" implies that the whole prayer, the energy by which we pray, is characterized by the nature of Christ, and that what we ask would be in agreement with the desires of our Lord!

Romans 14:7-12 reads,

> For none of us liveth to himself, and no man dieth to himself. For whether we live, we live unto the Lord; and whether we die, we die unto the Lord: whether we live therefore, or die, we are the Lord's. For to this end Christ both died, and rose, and revived, that he might be Lord both of the dead and living. But why dost thou judge thy brother? Or why dost thou set at nought thy brother? For we shall all stand before the judgment seat of Christ? For it is written, As I live, saith the Lord, every knee shall bow to me, and every tongue shall confess to God. So then every one of us shall give account of himself to God.

This passage shows us the constitution of all spiritual living! Spirituality is not in the action of one's life or his profession, but spirituality is the very motivation and conduct of that life toward the living God.

WHAT GOD VALUES MOST

The "works" that we have done in our minds and in the minds of others may seem noble and spiritual. But when these works are tested by God at the judgment seat of Christ, they may be burned up because the nature and character of such works were not in line with the nature of Christ. Those works depict our human nature acting out of us and for us. And so those works and deeds are burned up. Therefore, we should be careful that what we do is done in the name of (character of) Jesus. "And whatsoever ye do in word or deed, do all in the name of the Lord Jesus, giving thanks to God and the Father by him" (Colossians 3:17).

True spirituality can only be that which exists within a person by the presence and power of the Holy Spirit. No one can take on the character of Christ through his own determination. Only the Spirit of Christ indwelling the man can make him Christ-like!

"Exhort servants to be obedient unto their own masters, and to please them well in all things; not answering again; Not purloining, but shewing all good fidelity; that they may adorn the doctrine of God our Saviour in all things" (Titus 2:9-10).

I am to exhort you as laborers to be obedient to your employers. Please them! It has been said that many businesses are reluctant to hire Christians. The reason being that Christians have not performed well in the work force. When you work well and please your supervisors, then you are adorning the doctrine of God! What good is gospel preaching on the job if you are not doing your job as Christ would? Bad work performance hinders the gospel you preach. However, when Christians work hard, sacrificing to help their co-workers, striving to make the work environment more pleasurable, then they have an opportunity to share the gospel with those who want to listen! People know how Christians should act, and when your nature is Christ-like people are going to listen.

GOD CREATED MAN AND COMMANDS HIM TO DO TEMPORAL WORK

Ephesians 4:28 reads, "Let him that stole steal no more: but rather let him labour, working with his hands the thing which is good, that he may have to give to him that needeth." You are to bring in an income. You are to be profitable for society and man. The spiritual man views his work as a means of receiving money to help those who are in need. That is one of the purposes of your work. God expects you to be generous with your money by contributing to His church and the needy.

GOD PROMISES TO REWARD PEOPLE IN EVERYDAY JOBS

God promises to reward all work that is done in His name. This includes "secular" work. Secular work is typically defined as any occupation that is not considered ministry, such as: teaching school, working as white collar or blue collar professionals, and working in other professional positions. We typically treat secular work as something insignificant in eternal matters; it simply helps us pay the mortgage, the car note, and put food on the table. But if we were to have a spiritual mentality about our secular jobs and understand how God is using us in them, then we would understand that God promises to reward us for faithfully performing these jobs in the name of Jesus!

> "Servants, be obedient to them that are your masters according to the flesh, with fear and trembling, in singleness of your heart, as unto Christ; Not with eye service, as menpleasers; but as the servants of Christ, doing the will of God from the heart; With good will doing service, as to the Lord, and not to men: Knowing that whatsoever good thing any man doeth, the same shall he receive of the Lord, whether he be bond or free. And, ye masters, do the same things unto them, forbearing threatening: knowing that your Master also is in heaven; neither is there respect of persons with him" (Ephesians 6:5-9).

> "Servants, obey in all things your masters according to the flesh; not with eyeservice, as menpleasers; but in singleness of heart, fearing God: And whatsoever ye do, do it heartily, as to the Lord, and not unto men; Knowing that of the Lord ye shall receive the reward of the inheritance: for ye serve the Lord Christ" (Colossians 3:22-24).

God is telling you that secular work does matter in eternity! God promises to reward you if you do a good job. If you do your job with all your heart as unto the Lord, if you adorn God's doctrine by hard and faithful work, if you demonstrate integrity and character, then God is going to reward you in eternity.

God does not tell us to perform our jobs until we can really do something that counts for His kingdom. God is not suggesting that we leave jobs. He does not command everyone to go into the ministry of evangelism. He is not suggesting that everyone become the pastor of a church or a career missionary. Not everyone is called to those areas of service.

Instead, God is freeing people by giving assurance that He has placed them in strategic locations. What I am trying to assure you of is simply this: You can be spiritual in your secular job if you have the nature of Christ working through your life. And God promises to reward you in eternity for your faithfulness.

We assume that God values the work that is for eternity, not the work that is temporal. By this measure the work of ministers has eternal value because they deal in "spiritual" things and a common laborer or a shoe salesman is limited in his heavenly reward because such jobs are "temporal." But God does not place this type of measure on His people!

I believe the reason God chose Elisha over those studying to be prophets was because of his diligence in his secular job. This is a pattern in the Word of God. God did not choose great men and women who were grown up in ministry or trained for ministry to impact society. Instead He chose carpenters, fishermen, tax collectors, and shepherds. These were people who worked hard. People who worked days, nights, and overtime – these were the men that Jesus chose! He did not choose the Pharisees, Sadducees, and scribes- those who were refined in religious culture. Even so today, He chooses those who know how to work hard. If people do not work hard in the secular world they are not going to work hard in the ministry!

Let me illustrate this by the example that Jesus set: Can you imagine God on His knees washing dirt? Please keep in mind the context of what is going on and the significant action that Jesus takes. Imagine the circumstances surrounding the night of betrayal and the arrest of Jesus. On the way to the upper room the disciples are arguing with one another as to who is the greatest. Jesus is leaving them tomorrow. He has invested over three years into their lives. This is His last night to somehow make them understand, for they will assume the responsibility of His ministry.

If you were Jesus what would you do? Perhaps preach your greatest message or bring a severe rebuke. Maybe manipulate them and lay the heavy load of "duty" and "responsibility" upon them by saying, "I am really counting on you for the work that is ahead." But Jesus takes a course of action that many would not consider "spiritual."

> Jesus knowing that the Father had given all things into his hands, and that he was come from God, and went to God; ⁴He riseth from supper, and laid aside his garments; and took a towel, and girded himself. ⁵After that he poureth water into a basin, and began to wash the disciples' feet, and to wipe *them* with the towel wherewith he was girded. ⁶Then cometh he to Simon Peter: and Peter saith unto him, Lord, dost thou wash my feet? ⁷Jesus answered and said unto him, What I do thou knowest not now; but thou shalt know hereafter. ⁸Peter saith unto him, Thou shalt never wash my feet. Jesus answered him, If I wash thee not, thou hast no part with me. ⁹Simon Peter saith unto him, Lord, not my feet only, but also *my* hands and *my* head. ¹⁰Jesus saith to him, He that is washed needeth not save to wash *his* feet, but is clean every whit: and ye are clean, but not all. ¹¹For he knew who should betray him; therefore said he, Ye are not all clean. ¹²So after he had washed their feet, and had taken his garments, and was set down again, he said unto them, Know ye what I have done to you? ¹³Ye call me Master and Lord: and ye say well; for *so* I am. ¹⁴If I then, *your* Lord and Master, have washed your feet; ye also ought to wash one another's feet. ¹⁵For I have given you an example, that ye should do as I have done to you. ¹⁶Verily, verily, I say unto you, The servant is not greater than his lord; neither he that is sent greater than he that sent him. ¹⁷If ye know these things, happy are ye if ye do them (John 13:3 – 17).

The most important message Jesus could give His disciples that last night was not teachings on the resurrection, or teachings on miracles, or how to take your city for God. The thing they must know is humility. By being the example, Jesus shows His disciples that His work will succeed if they are in their right place. This place is not above people but beneath people. In essence, Jesus was saying, "I cannot use a haughty Peter. I cannot use an arrogant Matthew. I do not need a John who puts himself above the people."

God does not want you in a place where everybody serves you, but rather where it becomes your joy and delight to serve other people. This is the humble heart. This is the godly heart. This is the life that God can speak through and use. What is important in the kingdom of heaven and most beneficial to God's eternal plan is that we are going to serve God and man.

The role Jesus assumed that night (washing the disciples' feet) was the role of the lowest servant among the slaves. Jesus, knowing the contention his disciples have been involved in, realizes that He must provide a drastic illustration. He moves and takes a towel, a basin of water, and the dirty feet of His disciples. He then illustrates the most important lessons of His kingdom: Don't be selfish; love God and man more than you do yourself. And do not think more highly of yourself than you should.

The true test of our service is not that we do these things but the nature in which we do them. You see, Jesus was showing us the secret of joy. He was saying that when we do things like this it is then that we are acting most like Him. But the most important thing is the nature of how we serve. Many will serve religiously and perform their actions with a false piety and others will serve grudgingly.

Man's nature will not be happy washing dirty feet. Man's nature will not be happy putting others first. For example, at work you sacrifice to help a co-worker and they get the advancement over you. You know it was your help that caused them to get the recognition. Your flesh tells you that it is not fair! You can test whether it is the real nature of Christ in you that is responding by whether you have joy or not. Jesus shows us the most significant things in life are not the big things we consider to be "spiritual" but the common things. True spirituality is taking advantage of the common things God gives us to do every day – that is the mind-set of the spiritual person.

You may think the spiritual person is the one who walks into the pulpit of your church on Sundays. But there might be nothing spiritual about that person. The spiritual person is not necessarily the one who goes on the mission trips. Many people can get psyched up for such a trip.

The most spiritual may be the person that is seldom in the spotlight. He never preaches, he never teaches; yet everyday he lives before God. Everyday he goes to his job. He punches in on time. He works really hard as unto the Lord. He is admired and has favor with man. He is adorning the gospel of God with such beauty that people want to know the hope that he has in the Lord. He is faithful and diligent. He has lived before God in prayers and fastings. He demonstrates Christ in all his behaviors - that is the spiritual person! He is able to reveal Christ in the simple and mundane duties of daily life. It is not when we walk on water but when we see the basins of water behind the door, and we take the towel and serve somebody!

In August of 1930, forty-five-year-old Joseph Crater waved good-bye to friends after an evening meal in a New York restaurant, flagged down a taxi, and rode off. He was never seen or heard from again. After fifty years there has been no definitive explanation as to his demise. Because of his high exposure as a New York Supreme Court judge, some have suspected murder. Others suggest kidnapping or perhaps Mafia infringement. But most seem to think that suicide is the only explanation because a search of his apartment revealed one clue. A note was attached to a check, and both were left for his wife. The check was for a sizable amount, and the note simply read, *"I am very weary. Love, Joe."*

Weariness is tough- not the physical weariness that comes with mowing the lawn or the mental weariness that follows a hard day of decisions and thinking, but the weariness that comes just before you give up. It's the dispirited father, the abandoned child, or the retiree with time on his hands. It's that stage in life when motivation disappears; the children grow up, a job is lost, a wife dies. The result is weariness – deep, lonely, frustrated weariness.

Real spirituality is found in the person who can live the life of Christ in the midst of that kind of weariness. When everyone else is giving up, committing suicide, or sinking into meaningless despair; the spiritual take the towel, and on the wings of joy they soar above it all by living Christ in each and every day!

It does not matter how many people they preach to or if their name is on the marquee, or how many people are promoting them or how many millions of books they have sold or how many radio and

TV stations they are on. None of that matters because these accomplishments come through good human effort and showmanship! Yet how many of God's children are so awestruck by these modern day celebrities wishing it could be them. You can almost hear their thoughts, "Oh God I want to do something like that for you because I want to make an impact on eternity." But God is telling us, "If you really want to further My kingdom and make My name great in the earth, then follow my example. Take a bowl of water and a towel, humble yourself before men and God, and do unto others what you would have them do unto you. In the spirit of Christ help someone! Live where I have put you in life. Be spiritual in all you do and with whatever I have entrusted to you." Make others great! Don't step on other people! Be hospitable!

> If a brother or sister be naked, and destitute of daily food, [16]And one of you say unto them, Depart in peace, be *ye* warmed and filled; notwithstanding ye give them not those things which are needful to the body; what *doth it* profit? (*James 2: 15-16*).

> But whoso hath this world's good, and seeth his brother have need, and shutteth up his bowels *of compassion* from him, how dwelleth the love of God in him? (*1 John 3:17*).

Most Christians will live their entire lives having never raised the dead. Most will never walk on water. Most will never speak to a large crowd of people. Most will never see thousands of people come to Christ as a result of their preaching ministry. But if you do what God has called you to do, even if it is in the secular field, you will be rewarded as well.

Anybody can do the things that please God: Feeding the hungry, clothing the naked, ministering to the needy, and preaching the gospel to the poor. What an impact. You don't need the elaborate.

David was most like Christ, not when he faced down Goliath; but when he was holding a piece of Saul's clothing. When David, running for his life from King Saul-his friend turned enemy- encountered the sleeping king and used his knife, not as a weapon to kill the powerful king, but used it simply to cut, from the sleeping king's garment, a piece of cloth!

One of the greatest things Jesus did was to go through Samaria to meet an outcast woman at a well to give her eternal life! Jesus took the common things: the towel, the basin of water, and the dirty feet of arrogant men. With these He showed us that if we lived our lives in His name then that is spiritual, and He will reward us for it.

If you are working a secular job then do it with all your might and adorn the doctrine of God. Don't think that going to your job Monday through Friday and working overtime is un-spiritual. Your life today can have a major impact on your future with God. If you serve in the name of Jesus, then your actions will glorify God as much as the mightiest preacher in the largest congregation!

It is not simply the feats of great men that hold us, but the scars. We love Him because He first loved us!

CHAPTER 2

THE MAN OF GOD

… he shall be a vessel unto honour, sanctified, and meet for the master's use, *and* prepared unto every good work.

- The Apostle Paul to his friend Timothy

The Bible speaks of a man in Christ, but it also speaks of the man of God. The two are different. The man in Christ can become a man of God through obedience and discipline. The man of God will be consistent in his walk with God: giving, praying, and attending church. To be a man of God does not imply that one must become a pastor, evangelist, prophet, apostle, or teacher. Just because someone holds the office of an evangelist does not make him a Man of God; the office itself does not make a man of God. God produces such men from those who are diligently seeking Him.

By human measurements, religion has set standards regarding spiritual status and significance which most people sitting in our congregations will never attain. One of those measurements is that a man of God must be in full-time ministry, such as a pastor or evangelist. Such a standard is disastrous and discouraging because most believers will never be called to an office in the Body of Christ.

Because of these standards many in Christ will be overlooked for their value among God's people. Their valuable contributions and spirit-anointed life will not be appreciated, and a valuable work of God, which could come through them, is neglected.

It is my desire to encourage the lay person in Christ, that the life he lives can be used for eternal purposes even though he is not called to a specific office. I long for the layman to be excited about going to his job everyday knowing that it is his mission field, and he is reaping eternal rewards for Jesus Christ.

A true Christian is one who has died out of this present evil world. He has no more to do with it than Christ. He is dead to the law – dead to sin: alive in Christ – alive to God. He belongs to Heaven. His religion, his politics, his morals are all heavenly. He is a heavenly man walking on the earth … the Christian is not a monk, an ascetic, or a hermit. He is in the world but not of it. He is in the body, as to the fact of his condition; but not in the flesh as to the principle of his standing. He is a man in Christ.

The standing is fixed and unalterable. The state may graduate between the two extremes presented in the epistles. His state may graduate between two extremes. A Christian may be in the third heaven, amid the seraphic visions of that blessed and holy place; or he may, if not watchful, sink down into all the gross and evil things from which he was once delivered. C.H. Mackintosh.

If a man is determined to be a man of God he will choose to walk in heavenly places, rather than carnal places. In Paul's epistles to Timothy, two types of believers are revealed: the man in Christ and the man of God. All who are in Christ are saved and enjoy the benefits of redemption; however, a man in Christ can be a vacillating man. He will experience glorious things from the presence of God. One week he may be walking in the third heaven; his prayers seem to be answered immediately. God is talking with him. He knows that he is saved. He is ready to take on anything; nothing can stop him. However, a week later he is the most depressed man you ever met. He is questioning his salvation. Instead of being unstoppable, the smallest things in life are defeating him. He is vacillating between two extremes.

The man of God is different; he is living a higher life. His life is disciplined and therefore he enjoys a very blessed life. God intends for all His children to become mature and intimate with Him. He longs for all believers to experience the joy of His redemption.

TO BE IN CHRIST IS OF ABSOLUTE SIGNIFICANCE

I want to be very clear on the following point. I believe that all who are "in Christ" will experience the work of God in their lives. They will experience the process of sanctification; they will grow and mature. All who are in Christ are very significant. To be in Christ is the absolute blessing of God for all men. There is no greater place for anyone to be! However, many who claim to be in Christ, and God knows if they truly are, reap very little benefit from the vast wealth of redemption. Why is this? Perhaps it is because they fail to exercise themselves in the things of God. All of the joy is there for those who are in Christ, but they must avail themselves of that treasure by faith. Some who fail to reap the benefits believe that it all just comes automatically. But Paul said we are to work out our salvation ... for it is God who works in us ....

As I stated earlier, I desire for you to have the reality of this life. If you are in Christ then all of the promises and potentials of God are awaiting you. So when I speak of the man in Christ as vacillating, it is not to impugn the believer but to reveal that it is possible for some of God's children to neglect the benefits of redemption. My purpose in explaining Paul's letter to Timothy is not to put down anyone in Christ. I want to encourage you to possess the life that Jesus died to give you. If anyone is to be a man of God he must first be in Christ.

EXAMINING A MAN OF GOD

1 Timothy 3:1-5 presents the requirements for bishops,

> This *is* a true saying, If a man desire the office of a bishop, he desireth a good work. A bishop then must be blameless, the husband of one wife, vigilant, sober, of good behaviour, given to hospitality, apt to teach; Not given to wine, no striker, not greedy of filthy lucre; but patient, not a brawler, not covetous; One that ruleth well his own house, having his children in subjection with all gravity; (For if a man know not how to rule his own house, how shall he take care of the church of God?)

These requirements reveal a distinction between the average believer and those who will go on to be men of God. Perhaps not all of God's people have such a desire for godliness, but if a man is to lead among God's people then of necessity he must be a man of God.

The contrast between a man in Christ and the man of God are revealed here. For example, verse 6 says that a person who is in Christ may be a novice. By referring to a "novice" the Holy Ghost is not simply describing one who is beginning a life in Christ. A novice also refers to one who is unfit because he lacks experience. He lacks experience because of neglect. He has neglected the opportunities God has given him to learn.

A man can be in Christ for fifty years and still be a novice because he never learned through his trials or persecution; he never changed. He went into the persecution as a baby and came out as a baby – kicking and screaming, crying and complaining.

The novice is lifted up with pride. He would fall into the condemnation of the devil. He is not ruled by the spirit of God. He does not possess meekness. He is ruled by his lust. Giving him an office would ruin him. He would be lifted up with pride: wanting people to look up to him because he is a "bishop." He desires for people to see him as somebody important or special, he feels that he is above other people.

In contrasting the novice with the man of God, Paul says,

Till I come, give attendance to reading, to exhortation, to doctrine. Neglect not the gift that is in thee, which was given thee by prophecy, with the laying on of the hands of the presbytery. Meditate upon these things; give thyself wholly to them; that thy profiting may appear to all. Take heed unto thyself, and unto the doctrine; continue in them: for in doing this thou shalt both save thyself, and them that hear thee (1 Timothy 4:13-16).

There are specific terms used here to describe the Man of God-terms such as "continuing." He does not stop. He does not give up. He continues in the right way.

A man in Christ may not continue; he may faint in his prayer life. A man in Christ may be with the church on one Sunday and not be seen again for weeks. The man in Christ may faint in good works.

The man of God is going to continue in the Spirit. He knows the course that has been set and nothing is going to stop him.

To further describe the difference between the man of God and the man in Christ, Paul brings us to 1 Timothy 3 and 4. Chapter 3 points out things the man of God is doing. It refers to his fruit. Chapter 4 points out how that character was developed and how the fruit was produced in a mature man.

If we examine chapter 3 only, then we may possibly conclude that the man of God is identified by the works that he performs. One may conclude that if he were to be a man of God then he must simply "do" the right things: rule your house, do not be greedy, have a good reputation, be hospitable. But chapter 4 shows what produces that man. He loves the Word of God and doctrine. To be a man of God there must be a love for the Word of God. Many in the house of God do not love His word. They like truth, but they don't like sound truth. They like the preacher's sermon and what he reveals through his studies, but they do not like to study for themselves. They would prefer that the Sunday school teacher do all the studying, and then simply relate to them what the Bible says.

THE PREPARATION OF A MAN OF GOD

Chapter 4 explains the preparation of a man of God. The man of God does not neglect his gift or calling. He gives attention to it. He understands that he has a responsibility to God. God has chosen him. God has saved him. God has filled him with the Holy Ghost and has given him a calling in life. He may not be a pastor or missionary. He may work a secular job, but he is called and he knows it; he does not ignore that calling. He will exercise his gifts to be skillful and responsible for the Lord's kingdom. Many in the Body of Christ neglect their gifts. And because one neglects his gift, he is unskillful in the use of that gift and the work of God. What God had intended for that negligent believer is greatly hindered by a lack of preparation. On the other hand, the man of God gives himself to his gifts and callings. He longs to see all within his fellowship experiencing the joy of God's empowering life within.

Furthermore, the man of God wants people in the Body of Christ to see his growth and maturity in Jesus Christ. The Body of Christ sees a man who is diligent in the Word of God. The Body is blessed by the knowledge and application of the Word of God coming through his life: his ability to live the Word, to apply the Word, and to rightly divide the Word. People see his gifts. He is ministering to the Body. The man of God is encouraging others to grow in Christ, and he is not even the pastor! People see him and they say, "That is a man of God."

The man of God takes heed to himself. He knows that he can vacillate like other Christians. He understands his need for God's grace; he knows how he would revert to fleshly living without God. He looks at himself. He examines himself. He discerns his own heart. He continues in what is right, and by that he saves others. His life in Christ becomes a blessing to others. Every man should live an exemplary life in his home, to his wife and children. Every woman should follow the same example in her home, to her husband and children, and to her friends. Every church member should also strive to be an example to the church.

In 1 Timothy 6:3-5 we are shown a man who I would not consider to be a believer. However, he is found in the house of God. He has a form of godliness. He is among the people of God.

Do you know the most dangerous thing Noah faced once the floods came? Noah was safe and protected from everything that was going on outside the ark. The problems that Noah faced were all the problems inside the ark. Consider the wood pecker. The greatest obstacle for Noah was the wood pecker constantly pecking. That is the way it is in the Church. We are saved from everything outside the Church, the things in the world and the judgment upon the world. The greatest problems that church people face are from those inside the church, the little wood peckers that constantly peck and stir things up and murmur and complain, doting and saying, "Well I have some questions about the pastor." or, "I am suspicious of that brother over there."

So also, this person mentioned in 1 Timothy 6 is among the people of God, but he does not consent to the words or the doctrines of the church. He, like some church members today, is proud, unlearned, and doting. Doting means to be taken with a morbid interest in a thing as is tantamount to a disease. To "dote" means to be unable to let something go; you cannot be free of it. Sure it is a question you want answered, but it is a foolish question. You cannot let go of it. Do you always have to be doting over this same issue? Can you not see that your morbid interest in these foolish things has caused so much division and strife among God's people?

This man of 1 Timothy 6 is greedy and selfish. He believes that the evidence of godliness is in the accumulation of physical wealth and possessions.

In contrast, the man of God is revealed in *1 Timothy 6:6-12*. Paul states:

> … Godliness with contentment is great gain. [7]For we brought nothing into *this* world, *and it is* certain we can carry nothing out. [8]And having food and raiment let us be therewith content. [9]But they that will be rich fall into temptation and a snare, and *into* many foolish and hurtful lusts, which drown men in destruction and perdition. [10]For the love of money is the root of all evil: which while some coveted after, they have erred from the faith, and pierced themselves through with many sorrows. [11]But thou, O man of God, flee these things; and follow after righteousness, godliness, faith, love, patience, meekness. [12]Fight the good fight of faith, lay hold on eternal life, whereunto thou art also called, and hast professed a good profession before many witnesses.

The man of God is content. The man of God does not seek selfish gain. This does not mean he is not blessed. Nor does it mean that the man of God must take a vow of poverty. It simply means that the man of God does not pursue the world's treasures because he is content with God.

The man of God follows peace, love, meekness, and righteousness. He is looking for love. He is looking for righteousness. He is looking for meekness. When He finds it he joins himself to it. He wants his life to be one that builds up people in love. He lives to bring peace and not division. He fights the good fight of faith.

Consider the portrait of the man of God in 2 Timothy 2:10, 15-16,

Therefore I endure all things for the elect's sakes, that they may also obtain the salvation which is in Christ Jesus with eternal glory. ...Study to show thyself approved unto God, a workman that needeth not to be ashamed, rightly dividing the word of truth. But shun profane *and* vain babblings: for they will increase unto more ungodliness.

The man of God endures all things, not just some things. When someone says, "I can endure anything except what you do to my family. I cannot endure that." Then they are setting up a roadblock to becoming a man of God. Or when someone says, "I can endure anything except this." or, "I can endure being misunderstood, but I cannot endure slander to my reputation and talk behind my back!" These attitudes and exceptions prevent one from becoming a man of God.

Paul said a man of God endures all things for the sake of the church. It doesn't mean he likes it, but he keeps on walking in what is right by trusting God for the final outcome.

Again, in 2 Timothy 2 we find that all in the Body of Christ are not men of God. Consider verse 21:

If a man therefore purge himself from these, he shall be a vessel unto honour, sanctified, and meet for the master's use, *and* prepared unto every good work.

Clearly there is a contrast here between the vacillating Christian and the man of God. You find a person who does not have honor. Paul told Timothy that if one is to be beneficial to the kingdom of God then he must flee youthful lust. The fact that Paul would have to tell the believer to flee youthful lusts further proves that there are people in the Body of Christ who have not fled youthful lust. Youthful lust includes being childish, fussy, irritable, easily set off, inconsiderate of others. There are people in the Body of Christ in that state and they cannot be used effectively by God.

If everything is going their way then they will be fine. But if that childish person runs into anything difficult, anything uncomfortable such as somebody speaking against their reputation; then the child-ishness comes out. At that moment you cannot count on them. They quit. They cry. They sulk. They are unprofitable! Therefore the man of God is somebody who has fled youthful lust.

The man of God understands that people are going to talk about him. Difficult trials are going to come, and he is prepared for them all by the grace of God. He knows that all are not going to like him, and some may want to kill him; but he knows he has a life to live. He knows that the Holy Ghost is in him, and he is responsible to God for the life he lives. He knows there is victory and glory for God on the other side of all tests and trials.

The man of God avoids all things that bring strife. He is patient. He is apt to teach. He is gentle and meek. He instructs those who oppose themselves. He does not rebuke them; he instructs them. He comes with humility when he sees others going into sin or danger; he teaches them the things of Christ hoping they will be rescued from the danger ahead.

The man of God lives by the Word of God. The third significant time great weight is laid upon the study, understanding, and guid-ance of God's Word as it relates to the believers life is found in 2 Timothy 3:14-17:

> But continue thou in the things which thou hast learned and hast been assured of, knowing of whom thou hast learned *them*; And that from a child thou hast known the Holy Scriptures, which are able to make thee wise unto sal-vation through faith which is in Christ Jesus. All scripture *is* given by inspiration of God, and *is* profitable for doctrine, for reproof, for correction, for instruction in righteousness: That the man of God may be perfect, thoroughly furnished unto all good works.

Any believer seeking to mature in Christ is going to grow by the Word of God. Now many know God's Word, but few live by it. Growing by God's Word is not simply accomplished by the attaining of knowledge nor by the ability to provide the right scripture to a particular circumstance. The most important thing for a maturing man is that he is furnishing himself; he is equipping himself because he is living it. For example, the man of God is dealing with conflict in a particular friendship. God is telling him to forgive. His flesh does not want to forgive. However, the Bible teaches forgiveness; so he forgives! Suppose someone at work is needing assistance. He knows he should help, but he is stretched for time. Then he hears God telling him to go the second mile. The Bible teaches this so that is what he does. Or consider a situation at work. Others are being promoted above him, and he is being treated unfairly because he is a Christian. Within himself, he wants to put pressure on the company, perhaps levy some legal threat to the employer. Then the Bible speaks to him and says, "Vengeance is mine, I will repay, says the Lord." He understands that this is a word from God for him. So he obeys the Word and puts the matter into God's hand.

The man of God lives by the Word. He does not try to find a reason for doing something other than what the Bible teaches. However, many "Christians" excuse themselves from obeying the Word of God by saying, "Well, my situation is different. God will understand."

This last characteristic of the man of God is that he preaches the Word.

> Preach the word; be instant in season, out of season; reprove, rebuke, exhort with all longsuffering and doctrine. For the time will come when they will not endure sound doctrine; but after their own lusts shall they heap to themselves teachers, having itching ears; And they shall turn away *their* ears from the truth, and shall be turned unto fables. But watch thou in all things, endure afflictions, do the work of an evangelist, make full proof of thy ministry (*2 Timothy 4: 2-5*).

His life is consistent. You can count on him. The man of God continues when no one else will. When the Word of God is not popular, he still preaches the Word. He watches and endures and works fulfilling his ministry!

The immature Christian can quit, give up, faint, withdraw, and forsake the fellowship. But a man of God will not quit! Perhaps nobody likes him right now. Many have lost confidence in him, but he continues on.

The man of God has to work on amid all sorts of difficulties, trials, sorrows, disappointments, obstacles, questions, and controversies. He has his path to tread, his work to do. Come what may, he must serve. The enemy may oppose; the world may frown; the Church may be in ruins around him; false brethren may thwart, hinder, and desert; strife, controversy, and division may arise and darken the atmosphere; still the Man of God must move on regardless of all these things, working, serving, testifying, according to the sphere in which the hand of God has placed him and according to the gift bestowed upon him...

'Wherefore I put thee in remembrance that thou stir up the gift of God, which is in thee by the putting on of my hands.' The gift must be stirred up, else it may become useless if allowed to lie dormant ... it is not enough to possess a gift, we must wait upon the gift, cultivate it, and exercise it...

In the face of all this, the Man of God has to brace himself up for the occasion. He has to endure hardness; to hold fast the form of sound words; he has to keep the good thing committed to him; to be strong in the grace that is in Christ Jesus; to keep himself disentangled – however he may be engaged; he must keep himself free as a soldier; he must cling to God's sure foundation; he must purge himself from the dishonorable vessels in the great house; he must flee youthful lusts, and follow righteousness, faith, love, peace, with them that call on the Lord out of a pure heart. He must avoid foolish and unlearned questions. He must turn away from formal and heartless professors. He must be thoroughly furnished for all good works, perfectly equipped through a knowledge of the Holy Scriptures. He must preach the Word; be instant in season and out of season. He must watch in all things; endure afflictions; and do the work of an evangelist... C.H. Mackintosh.

CHAPTER 3

THE HOSPITALITY OF ONESIPHORUS RECEIVING PAUL'S REWARD!

"Now the end of the commandment is charity out of a pure heart, and *of* a good conscience, and *of* faith unfeigned..." (1 Timothy 1:5).

The Gospel proclaims pardon through the blood of the Lamb to every believing penitent sinner. The blood of Jesus redeems! The blood of Jesus delivers one from the past, the present, and all of the future. The blood of Jesus takes a person, and through His cross, puts an end to the old, condemned life and brings up a brand new life. "And the grace of our Lord was exceeding abundant with faith and love which is in Christ Jesus" (1 Timothy 1:14).

The person who has received this pardon can do nothing less than show this same mercy to every other sinner in the world, especially those of the household of faith. However, sometimes it appears that Christians seem to be more gracious and forgiving to the pagans rather than to fallen believers in their own churches. Rather than showing struggling believers grace and mercy, the tendency is to cast them aside, to be cold- hearted and bitter. After all, they have failed God! They brought reproach upon Jesus Christ. But the truth is that all believers will fail the body of Christ at some point. Maybe not to the degree or capacity of others, but there will be a time when even you experience failure. Somebody is going to find fault with you. And the fault they find will be true and accurate.

My point is this, if grace is to be displayed it must be displayed most effectively within the house of God. The people of the world are observing how we treat one another in the family of God. We can talk about the love of God. We can preach about the grace of God. But if the lost come into the church house and find anything but this love being demonstrated, then we will be exposed as frauds! If they find gossip, bitterness, dissention, and unloving people; then we will be considered hypocrites. Therefore, the end of the commandment is the demonstration of the love of God. According to the Holy Scripture this love is not the product of our own will power or self-power. This love is to come forth from us because He who is love lives in us! Adam Clarke says in his commentary:

> The end, aim, and design of God in giving this dispensation to the world is, that men may have an unfeigned faith, such as lays hold on Christ crucified and produces a good conscience from a sense of the pardon received, and leads on to purity of heart; love to God and man being the grand issue of the grace of Christ here below, and this fully preparing the soul for eternal glory. He whose soul is filled with love to God and man has a pure heart, a good conscience, and unfeigned faith. But these blessings no soul can ever acquire, but according to God's dispensation of faith.

"All that are with me salute thee. Greet them that love us in the faith. Grace be with you all. Amen" (Titus 3:15). Everyone that was in the faith had love one for another.

The Bible says that the Lord's servant must not gender strife, "But foolish and unlearned questions avoid, knowing that they do gender strifes. And the servant of the Lord must not strive; but be gentle unto all men" (2 Timothy 2:23-24).

If somebody is mistreating you and you want to be a servant of the Lord, then you have to be gentle in return. You cannot become what they are! The contrast to love is a heart or attitude that causes strife, complications, and dissention. Paul demonstrates this absence of love by describing one who is asking foolish questions. They bring up things they know are going to bring strife and become unprofitable. They are going to plant some suspicion about another in the church which is going to cause a division.

A person who has love wants to pull people together in Christ. Love to God and man is to be the grand issue of the grace of Christ. He whose soul is filled with love to God and man has a pure heart and a good conscience. This love of God is to spring out of a clean heart.

Barnes said in his commentary,

The Greek word agape (NT 26) means properly "love," affection, regard, good-will, benevolence. It is applied.
   a. To love in general.
   b. To the love of God and of Christ
   c. To the love which God or Christ exercises toward Christians (Rom 5:5; Eph 2:4; 2 Thess 3:5).
   d. The effect, or proof of beneficence, favor conferred (Eph 1:15; 2 Thess 2:10; 1 John 3:1).

PURE HEART

The heart is the place of one's will and emotions; the heart is the soul. It is what makes a particular person unique. It is from the heart that one possesses the ability to will, to think, and to act. The heart gives passion: it is what causes excitement; it is the instrument by which one loves and hates. When the end of the commandment states that love is out of a pure heart it simply means love flows out of one's heart. It is not something a person has to concentrate on giving. Love is something that flows out of the pure heart. If the heart is pure, the love that comes out of it will be pure. Love makes us check our heart: Is my motive pure? Is my desire pure? "Seeing ye have purified your souls in obeying the truth through the Spirit unto unfeigned love of the brethren, see that ye love one another with a pure heart fervently" (1 Peter 1:22).

Consider for a moment an impure heart that offers love. Say a person has a masterful ability to manipulate. Their actions of love are not pure; they have a selfish motive behind their actions. They will sacrifice, they will love, they will give; but their actions are not pure; there is a catch. So after they have sacrificed so much to help you, they now want you to be indebted to them. Be careful about your relationships. Some people do not call on the Lord out of a pure heart. They may be setting a trap for you. "Flee also youthful lusts: but follow righteousness, faith, charity, peace, with them that call on the Lord out of a pure heart" (2 Timothy 2:22). If you want your heart to be pure then the relationships you have with others must be pure also.

Love must be exercised; it has to be demonstrated. If you don't give the love away, then you become corrupt in your heart; and you consider the way of love to be the way of defeat.

Also, love must come from a good conscience.

GOOD CONSCIENCE

The conscience is the instrument the Holy Ghost uses to bring conviction into your life and heart. It is a judge. You know when you are violating your conscience. Your conscience can also bear witness with the Holy Ghost. A good conscience is one that has been cleared from guilt by sound faith in Christ. "Pray for us: for we trust we have a good conscience, in all things willing to live honestly" (Hebrews 13:18).

Have you ever acted nice, but at the same time your conscience was betraying you? You were saying things with your mouth that you did not believe in your heart, and your conscience was proclaiming you a hypocrite! Your conscience will let you know that your behavior is not in line with the faith of Christ. The faith of Christ is a real love and hospitality out of a pure heart and good conscience. Love with a good conscience is not a pretense. A good conscience does not let you do the "nice thing" while inside you are stewing over something about that person you befriended!

And lastly, this love can only come from a pure faith.

FAITH UNFEIGNED

Again Barnes explains the faith unfeigned as, "Undissembled confidence in God. This does seem to be intended specifically of faith in the Lord Jesus, but it means that all true love to God, such as this law would produce, must be based on confidence in him. How can anyone have love for one if he has no confidence in him? Can we exercise love to a professed friend in whom we have no confidence? Faith, then, is as necessary under the law as it is under the gospel."

The Jamieson, Fausset and Brown commentary explains, "Faith is feigned where there is not "good conscience." The false teachers drew men off from a loving, working, real, faith to profitless, speculative "questions" (1 Tim 1:4): they were just the opposite, "of corrupt minds," 1 Tim 6:5; "conscience seared," 1 Tim 4:2; Titus 1:15, "unbelieving;" "reprobate concerning the faith," 2 Tim 3:8: cf. Heb 3:12.

Charity is by definition acts of kindness, charitable works, and deeds for the benefit of others. God promises to reward these acts of love. God will not reward any act of love that comes out of an impure heart or a bad conscience or a feigned faith. Therefore, as I write about hospitality I am concerned that our actions will be rewarded by God. I would hate to consider that you lived a life of hospitality, and yet you go unrewarded on the judgment day.

GOD IS GOING TO GIVE OUT REWARDS

When you love out of a pure heart, God is going to reward you. He acknowledges your service.

"Now he that planteth and he that watereth are one: and every man shall receive his own reward according to his own labour" (1 Corinthians 3:8).

"And whatsoever ye do, do it heartily, as to the Lord, and not unto men; Knowing that of the Lord ye shall receive the reward of the inheritance: for ye serve the Lord Christ" (Colossians 3:23-24).

"Look to yourselves, that we lose not those things which we have wrought, but that we receive a full reward" (2 John 8).

HOW CAN WE OBTAIN REWARDS

Charge them that are rich in this world, that they be not high-minded, nor trust in uncertain riches, but in the living God, who giveth us richly all things to enjoy; That they do good, that they be rich in good works, ready to distribute, willing to communicate; Laying up in store for themselves a good foundation against the time to come, that they may lay hold on eternal life (1 Timothy 6: 17-19).

Let him that stole steal no more: but rather let him labour, working with his hands the thing which is good, that he may have to give to him that needeth (Ephesians 4:28).

God has given you a job. He blesses you in that job. He gives you an income and desires for you to live off of that income. He desires to bless you richly with all things for you to enjoy. He also wants you to understand that the high calling of your job is not simply to make money or climb the corporate ladder, but God has given you a job in order for you to be able to give to those in need.

WE CAN OBTAIN REWARDS BY MINISTERING TO THE LOST AND OUR ENEMIES

Now remember the way we do these acts of charity is by a pure heart of faith.

But I say unto you, Love your enemies, bless them that curse you, do good to them that hate you, and pray for them which despitefully use you, and persecute you; That ye may be the children of your Father which is in heaven: for he maketh his sun to rise on the evil and on the good, and sendeth rain on the just and on the unjust. For if ye love them which love you, what reward have ye? do not even the publicans the same? And if ye salute your brethren only, what do ye more than others? do not even the publicans so? Be ye therefore perfect, even as your Father which is in heaven is perfect (Matthew 5: 44-48).

Jesus wants you to be different. If you love only those who love you, then how are you different from everyone else? Therefore, love your enemies! By doing so you are able to do things others are not capable of doing because God lives in you. It is by this action of faith that you will be rewarded.

"But love ye your enemies, and do good, and lend, hoping for nothing again; and your reward shall be great, and ye shall be the children of the Highest: for he is kind unto the unthankful and to the evil. Be ye therefore merciful, as your Father also is merciful. Judge not, and ye shall not be judged: condemn not, and ye shall not be condemned: forgive, and ye shall be forgiven..." (Luke 6:35-37).

Your heart's first response should be mercy, not condemnation. Is that not the response you will want when fault is found with you? It is so easy to jump to judgment and condemnation. But the heart of God is one that is inclined toward mercy.

WE CAN OBTAIN REWARDS BY MINISTERING TO THE MINISTERS OF GOD

God promises many wonderful rewards for those who labor in His gospel. If you are not called to a particular office in the church, how can you receive these rewards? God is so wonderful that He gives all of us a way to share in the rewards of an office that one may never hold while on earth.

"He that receiveth you receiveth me, and he that receiveth me receiveth him that sent me. He that receiveth a prophet in the name of a prophet shall receive a prophet's reward; and he that receiveth a righteous man in the name of a righteous man shall receive a righteous man's reward. And whosoever shall give to drink unto one of these little ones a cup of cold water only in the name of a disciple, verily I say unto you, he shall in no wise lose his reward" (Matthew 10: 40 – 11:1). You can receive a prophet's reward just by receiving the prophet!

"For whosoever shall give you a cup of water to drink in my name, because ye belong to Christ, verily I say unto you, he shall not lose his reward" (Mark 9:41).

"By him therefore let us offer the sacrifice of praise   to God continually, that is, the fruit of our lips giving thanks to his name. But to do good and to communicate forget not: for with such sacrifices God is well pleased. Obey them that have the rule over you, and submit yourselves: for they watch for your souls, as they that must give account, that they may do it with joy, and not with grief: for that is unprofitable for you" (Hebrews 13: 15-17).

If you want to profit, obey those who have the rule over you. Submit to them. They are watching over your soul. These leaders will give an account to God for how they cared for you. So if you do not submit, who is going to have the problem? Not the one who is watching over your soul. Failing to submit will be unprofitable for you.

"Let him that is taught in the word communicate unto him that teacheth in all good things. Be not deceived; God is not mocked: for whatsoever a man soweth, that shall he also reap. For he that soweth to his flesh shall of the flesh reap corruption; but he that soweth to the Spirit shall of the Spirit reap life everlasting" (Galatians 6:6-8).

"Let the elders that rule well be counted worthy of double honour, especially they who labour in the word and doctrine. For the scripture saith, Thou shalt not muzzle the ox that treadeth out the corn. And, the labourer is worthy of his reward. Against an elder receive not an accusation, but before two or three witnesses" (1 Timothy 5: 17-19).

For it is written in the law of Moses, Thou shalt not muzzle the mouth of the ox that treadeth out the corn. Doth God take care for oxen? Or saith he it altogether for our sakes? For our sakes, no doubt, this is written: that he that ploweth should plow in hope; and that he that thresheth in hope should be partaker of his hope. If we have sown unto you spiritual things, is it a great thing if we shall reap your carnal things? If others be partakers of this power over you, are not we rather? Nevertheless we have not used this power; but suffer all things, lest we should hinder the gospel of Christ. Do ye not know that they which minister about holy things live of the things of the temple? and they which wait at the altar are partakers with the altar? Even so hath the Lord ordained that they which preach the gospel should live of the gospel" (1 Corinthians 9:9-14).

When someone is ministering the Word of God we should give to them. We must practice to appreciate the things of God. When you give it will be given back to you. When people say they are not being fed anymore or that they are not getting anything out of the message, I promise you it is because they have not been giving back. They have been indulging themselves in spiritual things without ever providing carnal things to those ministers! They are not giving. It is not the pastor's fault or the church's fault – it is their fault. They are not giving! When you give with a thankful heart expressing your appreciation for the man of God and the Word of God, then God receives your act of love and continues to bless you.

WE CAN OBTAIN REWARDS BY MINISTERING TO THE BODY OF CHRIST

"And let us not be weary in well doing: for in due season we shall reap, if we faint not. As we have therefore opportunity, let us do good unto all men, especially unto them who are of the household of faith" (Galatians 6: 9-10).

The important thing here is that we do not faint. If you are performing acts of hospitality hoping that others will always respond positively to you, I can assure you that you will faint. You are going to feel used. You will feel unappreciated. You gave encouragement, and they didn't receive it. You gave them money, and they didn't thank you. You will get frustrated and begin to quit.

Please do not spend your acts of charity hoping that man will reward you. Even good Christian people may overlook your sacrifice of hospitality. Serving and giving with the hope of man's recognition and reward can lead to great discouragement. You must rely upon God to reward.

"Therefore, my beloved brethren, be ye steadfast, unmovable, always abounding in the work of the Lord, forasmuch as ye know that your labour is not in vain in the Lord" (I Corinthians 15: 58-16:1).

"But, beloved, we are persuaded better things of you, and things that accompany salvation, though we thus speak. For God is not unrighteous to forget your work and labour of love, which ye have shewed toward his name, in that ye have ministered to the saints, and do minister. And we desire that every one of you do shew the same diligence to the full assurance of hope unto the end: That ye be not slothful, but followers of them who through faith and patience inherit the promises" (Hebrews 6: 9-12).

Little is known of Onesiphorus. But one thing that is known about him was the way he modeled the love of Christ. He so impressed the apostle Paul that the great apostle sought the blessings of God for Onesiphorus. To illustrate this fact, I think it would be profitable to see the example that Onesiphorus has left us:

> The Lord give mercy unto the house of Onesiphorus; for he oft refreshed me, and was not ashamed of my chain: [17]But, when he was in Rome, he sought me out very diligently, and found *me*. [18]The Lord grant unto him that he may find mercy of the Lord in that day: and in how many things he ministered unto me at Ephesus, thou knowest very well (2 Timothy 1:16 – 18).

The first thing we see is that Onesiphorus often refreshed the apostle. The work of the ministry is very hard and many are the hardships that come. Paul found comfort in Onesiphorus. Paul said that Onesiphorus relaxed him!

Second, the Apostle said that Onesiphorus was not ashamed of his chains. Others were ashamed of Paul. But Onesiphorus showed enduring friendship. Today Paul is justified, but not so during his life. He constantly suffered assault and false accusations. Many people, even Christians, were ashamed to be associated with Paul. But Onesiphorus had a love that conquered the opinions of man and loved the servant of God unashamedly.

Third, Paul said that Onesiphorus sought him out. This was not as easy as it may seem. Paul was often kept in secret because of the threats against his life. What Onesiphorus did was difficult; it cost him time – a commodity that many today are not willing to give!

Fourth, Paul said that Onesiphorus found him. When Paul is abandoned by most, locked up as a criminal, Onesiphorus risks everything to actually come to Paul.

Fifth, Onesiphorus' hospitality was open and public! Paul said in his letter that Timothy knew how well Onesiphorus had ministered to him. Love is the end of the commandment; love is the demonstration of saving faith, and Onesiphorus showed it to the whole world!

And the Holy Spirit says through the Apostle Paul of Onesiphorus that there will be mercy for him in the day of Christ. The Holy Spirit is promising to reward this faithful, loving servant! He didn't minister only when it was convenient. It was not an occasional thing. It was his life's habit.

So what if you just do good things from a heart that is not pure? You see, the purpose of this book is not simply to give you nice things to do. I wrote at great length about the pure heart because it matters how and why you do something good. You can be busy doing nice things, and yet your heart may be wrong. I want you to receive a full reward. I do not want your labor in Christ to be in vain. The Spirit of God is admonishing believers that He wants to reward us with a full reward.

CHAPTER 4

THE LORD IS MY HELPER

"*Let your* conversation *be* without covetousness; *and be* content with such things as ye have: for he hath said, I will never leave thee, nor forsake thee. So that we may boldly say, The Lord *is* my helper, and I will not fear what man shall do unto me" (Hebrews 13:5 – 6).

I want us to consider how we are to give – to be hospitable. A believer's lifestyle is to be different from unbelievers because the believer does not covet. Believers are to be content with the things they have because God will never leave nor forsake them (Hebrews 13:5)!

The believer's contentment is not in the things possessed. The believer is content "with" those things but not "in" those things. The true source of a believer's contentment is that God will never leave nor forsake him! Because of God's faithfulness the believer is content.

Believers should live in such a way and make do with the things that they have been given that they might boldly say, "The Lord is my helper" (Hebrews 13:6). Believers are free of covetousness and content because God is with them and will help in every situation. Because the Lord is our helper, we will be able to do so much, give so much, and help others; not because of our vast wealth but because of the blessing the Lord puts on our giving!

It is natural to think of our contentment in the physical possessions we have:

Wealth,

Talent,

Education....

As a result, so few do so little because they feel they have little to offer.

GOD IS WITH US

To properly understand the fact that God is with us and will be our helper it is necessary for us to see the context of the passage in Hebrews. The whole book of Hebrews shows how much better Jesus is than anything that has come before Him. In old times God spoke through Moses and the angels, but now God has spoken unto us by His son. Previously there was an Old Covenant, but now we have a better Covenant! Previously there was a priesthood, but now, with Jesus, we have a better priesthood. Abel's blood cried vengeance, but the blood of Jesus cries better things.

Hebrews is a comparison of what was and, now, what is by the coming of Jesus Christ, who is so much better. Hebrews gives details about the advantages that we now have because of Jesus. Hebrews describes our new access to God and the work that Jesus is performing on our behalf.

For example, Mr. Wigglesworth was so excited to encounter needs. He was so convinced of how complete he was in Christ. He believed that God was with him and would not forsake him. Smith Wigglesworth believed he contained the answer to every need with which he was confronted. In Jesus name he stepped out, and on that name and in faith he laid hold of the God who would help him!

As we come to Hebrews Chapter 11, we are told what ordinary men and women have accomplished by God. This chapter speaks of ordinary people who had an exceptional faith in the living God. The chapter is not about mighty people but a mighty God. We make of Moses more than he would make of himself. We do the same to Abraham, Elijah, Joshua, and the rest of those "heroes" of the faith. The sad result is that so many believers excuse their anemic Christianity by saying, "I am not Moses. I am not Abraham...." But none of these "heroes" of the faith were confident in their ability. They were so much like us today! Moses argued with God and insisted that God had the wrong man! When God sent for Gideon and said, "Thou mighty man of valor ...." Gideon's response was, "Who me?" It is clear that these men and women did not think of themselves in a great way; they thought of God in a great way. They went forth on the word of God, and God was faithful; great things were accomplished!

Now Hebrews 11 pushes us into Hebrews 12 where we are told that a great cloud of witnesses surrounds us. These witnesses testify that if we walk with God the way they walked with God, then we will experience the same faithful God.

Do not make excuses. Do not say why we cannot. Do not live in limitation. Live in faith! These witnesses are telling us that God answers prayer. God will work miracles in our lives. God will not fail us. God converts families. God causes the enemy to run in fear. God has healed, delivered, and rescued. Therefore, believe!

Our contentment is not in things: money in the bank, a stockpile of shoes and clothes, food in the pantry. Our contentment is not in those things. Our contentment is in this fact, "... ye are come unto Mount Sion, and unto the city of the living God, the heavenly Jerusalem, and to an innumerable company of angels, To the general assembly and church of the firstborn, which are written in heaven, and to God the Judge of all, and to the spirits of just men made perfect, And to Jesus the mediator of the new covenant, and to the blood of sprinkling, that speaketh better things than that of Abel" (Hebrews 12:22-24).

This is what we have come to! You are a child of the great king! Your life is in heaven and heaven is your country! Because of this, "*Let your* conversation *be* without covetousness; *and be* content with such things as ye have: for he hath said, I will never leave thee, nor forsake thee. So that we may boldly say, The Lord *is* my helper, and I will not fear what man shall do unto me ... Jesus Christ the same yesterday, and today, and forever ... Now the God of peace, that brought again from the dead our Lord Jesus, that great shepherd of the sheep, through the blood of the everlasting covenant, Make you perfect in every good work to do his will, working in you that which is wellpleasing in his sight, through Jesus Christ; to whom *be* glory for ever and ever. Amen" (Hebrews 13:5, 8, 20-21).

REVEALING GOD IN OUR GIVING

Because we belong to God and His kingdom, He will never let us suffer lack. He will abound to us in grace and enable us to do His will, bringing Him glory in every situation. And when people see our good works they will wonder how we are able to accomplish so much.

The marvelous thing is when the world realizes that it is not great wealth, position, or worldly resources that enable us to accomplish great things; then we will be able to tell them, "The Lord is my helper." If we only accomplished what our wealth allowed, the world would never marvel at our accomplishments. But when God multiplies and blesses our resources then the world is astounded!

Contentment is not resting in what you have; that is what the world does. Contentment is a lifestyle of letting go and liberating ourselves from our possessions. We do not have to live worrying about things. That is the lifestyle of the Gentiles who do not know God. Yet how many believers today live in worry and fear of carnal things?

One of our greatest witnessing tools is the way we live. God makes us complete in every good work to do His will, working in us that which is well-pleasing in His sight. This "good work" does not originate with us. It is not prompted because your pastor gave you a to-do-list of things that are benevolent or hospitable. Hospitality is not simply a discipline of doing good! Though modern church programs have come to this deplorable state, good works alone is not what God is after. Modern church programs are consumed with humanitarian efforts. These programs model the world, model the United Way, and model the twelve- step- program. These programs put Christian lingo into all its methods, and then call it acts of faith. But God is saying, "No. That is not the way it is supposed to be! It is supposed to be that good works flow from you because I am at work in you to do what is well-pleasing in my sight!" All the acts of hospitality are concluded by Jesus Christ being praised because he did marvelous and miraculous things through our lives.

The life of a true Christian should
SHOW THE WORLD GOD IS STILL BENEVOLENT.

You home school all day but still find a way to run to the store for the elderly. You bring them their medication and gladly help because the Lord is your helper. We can witness by saying, "It was a pleasure for me to cook the meal and bring it to your house; the Lord helped me do it!"

Our lives can leave people wondering, "How do you do so much for others? How do you take those mission trips? How do you give to the church like that?" And we can joyfully say, "Because the Lord is my Helper!"

We are the means by which all of God's acts of benevolence are to occur on earth. You are God's chosen vessel by which He wants to demonstrate His charity, kindness, and love to other believers and the lost that live around us. When you withhold those acts of kindness, you are restraining the Holy Spirit from bringing glory to Jesus Christ.

UNDERSTANDING COVETOUSNESS

You must understand covetousness this way. When Hebrews 13 tells us not to be covetous, we immediately begin to think that we are not to desire what someone else has. We think coveting is comparing our possessions to others, wishing we had what they possess. Though that is covetousness, the idea in Hebrews 13 is more involved. Covetousness is revealed in a believer's life when he holds on to what God has given him rather than liberally sharing it with those that are in need. If you cannot share what God has given, if you cannot give your tithes and offerings, then you are covetous! It does not matter that you are content with your bank account, and you want nothing more than what you have. If you hold on to what you have, you are being greedy; you are coveting.

This doesn't mean that you give all your money and time away. I am not suggesting that you deplete your bank account. You are to first provide for your family. You are to pay your house bill, your utilities, and so forth. To neglect these responsibilities in the name of ministry is to put God to the test! From what God allows us to have in surplus, we should be willing to give, serve, and share as the Holy Spirit reveals to us various needs.

Our lifestyle is to be blessed beyond compare. If you want to squeeze out all the blessings and joy of the Christian life, you have got to grow up and learn to be a consistent and joyful giver! The people that dry up the quickest are those who stop giving. They do not allow the Holy Spirit to get through them the things that He has gotten to them. I am not only talking of money; I refer to gifts of grace, mercy, words of encouragement, and so forth. If you do not give what the Holy Spirit is giving you, the time will come when He stops giving to you. Then you will begin to dry up and become unhappy and bitter. The Holy Spirit will take what He was going to give you and give it to one He knows will use it for the glory of God.

If you want to live in the gifts of the Holy Spirit and see the gifts increasing in your life then start giving what you have! Quit whining about other believers who do little or nothing and do all you can do. Exercise the gifts and abilities that God has given you. Do not worry that others are not doing something; you do something!

The fact that all we have belongs to the Lord is hard for many believers to accept. They believe it is their money, their house, their job, and their car. When believers live in that mentality they are just like the world, full of covetousness.

Giving is an action designed into you by God; it's the air into which you were born! But until you realize that, you'll cling desperately to everything you have. Listen, "Whoever sows generously will also reap generously" (2 Corinthians 9:6).

Your seed is anything you can multiply:
    Love,
        Time,
            Money.

Your harvest is what comes back to you in benefits like:
    Joy,
        Relationships,
            Finances.

Don't pray for a generous heart; practice being generous and your heart will follow. As long as you're a sower, God will give you seed. If He's not giving you all the seed you want at the moment, maybe you haven't become a sower yet!

Practicing hospitality can be scary at first. We will fight doubts, "What if I do not have the money or the time? How can I do it?" But once we step out in faith and see how God really does help us, then we begin to fly; and life takes on its greater meanings.

People who never live are those who have lived always wishing they had more:

More Money,
More Intelligence,
More Influence.

Therefore they dream of the life they might have lived and the deeds they might have accomplished!

To this pointless attitude of fallen man, God says, "No!" He tells His children, "You have what is needed! I have given Myself to you!" Do not covet your possessions – be extravagant with what you have!

You see, you are doing things in the arena of life, and people are noticing. They are confused and begin asking, "How do you give ten percent of your money to the Lord?" Then you can respond, "Because the Lord is my helper!"

I have so many people tell me that they have no idea how they make it from month to month. But the one thing they know is that if they stopped tithing they would not make it! Yet so many believers sit back and take inventory: how much time do I have? How much money do I have? And they, not the Holy Spirit, determine their contributions based on those evaluations.

Let God tell you what He wants you to do, and then step out in faith and do it. Don't look into your bank book; look to Jesus and obey Him! Don't look at your investments; look at the poor!

IT IS THE BLESSING GOD PUTS ON OUR GIVING

It is not the amount given, but it is what God does with the things we put in His hands. When you give your offering to the Lord, although it may be small, He then blesses it. And it is amazing what God does with it.

Do not limit God because you think you do not have enough: I don't have enough money, I don't have enough Bible knowledge, I don't have enough time .... Give Him what you have! You may only be able to give a little. You may not be able to meet the total need, but if God helps you, He can totally meet the need with what you have given!

A little bread and a couple of fish blessed by Jesus can feed 5000! Moses with only a rod can open the sea! If David puts the five stones into God's hands, he can overcome the mighty Goliath. If the widow will give her last cake to the prophet in the name of God, then God will feed her, the boy, and the prophet until the famine ends!

Offer your gift to God and count on God!

Don't be covetous and hoard – Give!

Believe and say, "The Lord is my helper; I will not fear!"

CHAPTER 5

BLESSED FOR THE TESTIMONY OF GOD

Let your conversation *be* without covetousness; *and be* content with such things as ye have: for he hath said, I will never leave thee, nor forsake thee (Hebrews 13:5).

I rejoice that living faith is demonstrated in the common duties of life. According to James, feeding the hungry, giving water to the thirsty, and clothing the naked is how one can express that his faith is alive!

Faith is not demonstrated in the size of your house, the car you drive, or the size of your nest egg; faith is demonstrated in the way you portray the life of Jesus in the common activities of life.

Man can easily motivate himself to do something monumental: like going on a mission trip or joining a retreat. To prepare for these events we pray, fast, and walk after God. However, typically once the big event is over, most will revert to the lifestyle they lived prior to the preparation of that event: They will become occupied with their own agendas. Swamped by the demands of secular employment, they will pass the homeless on the streets or pass up suffering people in the hospitals while attending to their own business. What kind of faith is that? How is that faith any different from those who have no faith? What is so impressive about doing something for a week but failing the Lord the rest of the year?

God had rather see you being faithful everyday ... in the small things ... in the way you treat your spouse and children ... or even your enemies ... than simply to give Him one or two exceptional weeks a year!

True Christianity is revealed in how we live this life on a daily basis. Hospitality was expressed by Jesus on the night of His betrayal when He took the basin of water and washed the disciples' feet. This was His last night with them - the most important time of instruction. They had been fighting with each other, arguing about who was the greatest. And Jesus, in that last night, has to find a way to convince them of the life He is calling them to and what manner of men they are to be. So Jesus takes a basin of water and washes their feet! What a radical display of His kingdom! What an awesome show of truth! Jesus told them, "If you know what I have done to you, then you go and do likewise, and your joy will be full." Jesus demonstrated the practical issue of Christianity.

THE BELIEVER'S CONTENTMENT

Don't desire what other people have. Don't live wishing you had it. Don't live trying to scheme how you can get it. Our contentment is not found in wealth or the accumulation of possessions but in the fact that we have the Lord! If we have the Lord we have everything. We are of all people most wealthy! You might not have the latest appliances in your kitchen. You may not have the finest home. You may not drive a luxury car. Perhaps you deal with frequent maintenance on your worldly goods, but you have the living God in your life! God has committed Himself to you: He will feed you and care for you. God is going to deliver you. God will minister to you. Because God has promised never to leave nor forsake you, you are wealthy.

Because the Living God is your portion then you *cannot* be covetous. For a people to whom the Living God has committed Himself to be covetous would impugn the character of the God who has vowed to care for and satisfy them. Covetousness is to look upon the possessions of others desiring to make those possessions your own in order that your life will feel complete! Imagine a people whose God is the Lord living covetous lives as though God cannot satisfy them!

When a believer is free from covetousness he no longer entertains the excuse which says, "If I had what they had then I could really be hospitable. If I had their home I would have people over all the time and minister." One who is free from covetousness would no longer be embarrassed with the home that God has given him.

Believers must quit saying, "If I had their money I would minister and help the needy. If I had their job then I would be respected, but who am I that people should listen to me?" However, this is what happens to so many in the church when it comes to hospitality; they look at what they have and judge whether it is good enough to help the ministry of Jesus Christ.

God is not interested in material things. He is not interested in your home, your car – He is just interested in your heart. The hospitable person has a heart that wants to give; the hospitable person wants to demonstrate his wealth in Jesus. It is not important that you can get twenty people in your living room; maybe you can only fit two people around your dinner table - but you use what you have for the glory of God!

Our contentment lies in the fact that God is with us and will never forsake us; so, we might boldly say that the Lord is our helper! God wants us to live as though He is our God, demonstrating our faith everyday in such a way that we can say, "The Lord is my helper." You should give in such fashion that people wonder how you did it. How did you do that? How do you bring people into your home all the time? You have a job, you work, and yet you go on the mission field – how do you do it? You work all day and come home to your family and still find a way to prepare a meal for the sick – how do you do it? And you say, "The Lord is my helper!" How can you give to the homeless? The Lord helps me do it.

No one is richer or freer than the one who can take the things that Jesus has given and then give them away to the glory of God. You see, it is also covetous to hoard what belongs to you. God gives to you so that you can bless others. Your contentment is not that you have many possessions but that you have the Lord!

It is more blessed to give than to receive. The people that learn to give are able to receive. People who cannot receive do not give; they do not understand the principle of giving.

God be merciful unto us, and bless us; *and* cause his face to shine upon us; *Selah*

That thy way may be known upon earth, thy saving health among all nations. Let the people praise thee, O God; let all the people praise thee. let the nations be glad and sing for joy: for thou shalt judge the people righteously, and govern the nations upon earth. *Selah*

Let the people praise thee, O God; let all the people praise thee. *Then* shall the earth yield her increase; *and* God, *even* our own God, shall Bless *Us*. God shall bless us; and all the ends of the earth shall fear him (Psalms 67).

WHY WE WANT TO BE BLESSED

This is why we want to be blessed; it is not a selfish motivation: we want God to bless us and be merciful to us so that Jesus will be known on the earth and His saving health among the nations. People are going to visibly see how wonderful it is to belong to God. That is what our life is to express – how wonderful it is to belong to God: He saves, heals, and blesses!

The reason we should want to be blessed and the reason God wants to bless us is because of the testimony He is going to receive when His people are blessed. Because God is our contentment, and loves blessing us, we live praising God! We praise Him in good times and bad because we know that He is our God who will not forsake us!

God shows us in His word how His favor upon our lives can cause nations to fear Him. When Abraham fled to Abimelech's kingdom, out of fear, he instructed his wife Sarah to claim that she was his sister. Abraham feared that the men of Gerar would kill him to have Sarah. Abraham believed that the people of this kingdom had no fear of God, "…Because I thought, Surely the fear of God *is* not in this place; and they will slay me for my wife's sake" (Genesis 20:11).

Abimelech, because he thought Sarah was unwed, took her to himself. And here is where we see God working for His children and putting fear in the nations...

God came to Abimelech in a dream by night and said to him:

Behold; thou *art but* a dead man, for the woman which thou hast taken; for she *is* a man's wife. …And God said unto him in a dream, Yea, I know that thou didst this in the integrity of thy heart; for I also withheld thee from sinning against me: therefore suffered I thee not to touch her. Now therefore restore the man *his* wife; for he *is* a prophet, and he shall pray for thee, and thou shalt live: and if thou restore *her* not, know thou that thou shalt surely die, thou, and all that *are* thine. Therefore Abimelech rose early in the morning, and called all his servants, and told all these things in their ears: and the men were sore afraid. Then Abimelech called Abraham, and said unto him, What hast thou done unto us? and what have I offended thee, that thou hast brought on me and on my kingdom a great sin? (Genesis 20:3, 6-9).

God is telling Abimelech, "You are a dead man because you have another man's wife. You have the wife of the man I have chosen ... I have joined myself to ... and upon whom my face shines: I am blessing him, being merciful to him, and defending him." [Author's paraphrase]

Abraham was not righteous in his behavior. God even admits the fault of Abraham and acknowledges Abimelech's integrity. But because Abraham is in relationship with God, the Lord intervenes, preventing Abimelech from defiling Sarah.

Not long after, Abraham's son Isaac has an encounter with Abimelech: Isaac discovers the wells that his father once had. (The Philistines had destroyed the wells when Abraham died.) Isaac restores the wells. Now the men of Gerar begin to strive with Isaac claiming that the water belonged to them. Isaac leaves that place and restores another well. The men of Gerar run him off of that well also. But notice how God intervenes on his, Isaac's, behalf:

Then Abimelech went to him from Gerar ... and Phichol the chief captain of his army. ²⁷And Isaac said unto them, Wherefore come ye to me, seeing ye hate me, and have sent me away from you? ²⁸And they said, We saw certainly that the LORD was with thee: and we said, Let there be now an oath betwixt us, *even* betwixt us and thee, and let us make a covenant with thee; ²⁹That thou wilt do us no hurt, as we have not touched thee, and as we have done unto thee nothing but good, and have sent thee away in peace: thou *art* not the blessed of the LORD (Genesis 26:26-29).

This is amazing! When Isaac is run out of a country, the king and General of the Army go after Isaac because they can see he is the blessed of the Lord! This is one man against a nation! They are saying, "Listen we want to make a covenant with you; we do not want you to hurt us!"

What was their real fear? It wasn't Isaac. After all they kicked him out of the country. They were afraid because this was a man in relationship with the Living God – they feared Isaac's God. Abimelech wanted Isaac's assurance that his God would not hurt them!

We are to pray and desire the blessings of God upon our lives so that the nations fear God. It is confessed that the United States is a Christian nation. However, I do not recall a time when I have seen practical Christianity lived out in this great nation: not in politics, government, education halls, or even in its judicial system.

We have a nation that does not fear God. Just notice the shows on TV. They make fun of Christ, fun of the church, fun of the Lord. Accusations are hurled against the "right-wing" conservative Christian.

If God were really blessing His people, then perhaps there would be a fear in our country once again, and the country would come to us saying, "Forgive us for what we have been saying. We have seen that God is with you." Maybe the problem with America is that few people see the Living God in relationship with those who claim to be His people. But instead of our nation seeing believers praising God in good times and bad, they do not perceive any difference between their lives and the lives of those who claim to be in Christ! Christians suffer like the world and cry like the world. Christians despair like the world - despair as though they have no God to turn to.

But how different it would be if God's people began to praise Him and live for Him! Our nation could not help but notice the hand of God if believers would exercise a living faith in the daily routines of life and live crying out to God, "Oh God bless us that our nation will fear you."

WHAT IS THIS BLESSING

What is the blessing? It is God's presence! That God is with you is the blessing! God is joined to you and His face shines upon you; therefore, He is merciful to you, blessing you: when you go out, He will be there; when people rise up against you, He will stop them; when any weapon is formed against you, God will not allow it to harm you; when the enemy comes in like a flood, God will lift up a standard against them. And God is going to show the nation that there is a people who know their God.

As with Abraham, nations did not fear God because of some greatness on Abraham's part; they feared him simply because he had a relationship with God. And why were nations afraid of Isaac? The scriptures accredit him with no heroic act, not one miracle. But why was he blessed? God blessed him because of Abraham! Isaac has favor with God for Abraham's sake, "… I will be with thee, and will bless thee … I will perform the oath which I swear unto Abraham thy father; And I will make thy seed to multiply as the stars of heaven, and will give unto thy seed all these countries; and in thy seed shall all the nations of the earth be blessed; Because that Abraham obeyed my voice, and kept my charge, my commandments, my statutes, and my laws" (Genesis 26:3-5).

You may not even be aware of how God is blessing you! Abraham didn't know that Abimelech was having a dream that night. But God was blessing Abraham; God was speaking to Abimelech. God told Abimelech that he was a dead man if he did not treat Abraham right! You have no idea who God might be talking to this very night. Who has been giving you a hard time? Who has been persecuting you? Do not faint! Do not give up! You are blessed; God may be speaking in your behalf tonight! Perhaps God is telling them, "You are fooling around with my child; you are a dead man unless you stop!" You have no idea how the tables are going to turn tomorrow. You are blessed of the Lord.

If Isaac was blessed so much for Abraham's sake, then notice this: "Blessed *be* the God and Father of our Lord Jesus Christ, who hath blessed us with all spiritual blessings in heavenly *places* in Christ" (Ephesians 1:3).

If God is fully committed to Isaac - his preservation, his protection, the protection of his children, crops, cattle, and home - for Abraham's sake, then what is God's commitment to you for Jesus' sake?

God blessed Isaac because of Abraham; will He not bless you for Jesus? God turned armies away from Isaac; will He not move heaven and earth for you? God would not let anything frustrate what He promised to Isaac's father; can you not expect even more for Jesus' sake? All of Israel confessed they were blessed because of Abraham, Isaac, and Jacob! Israel expected those blessings. They anticipated them because of their relationship with Abraham, Isaac, and Jacob.

How much more is God committed to fulfilling those blessings in your life because of God's relationship with His Son, because of the promises He has made with His Son? If Isaac could be confident in God's providence because of Abraham, surely you can be confident in God's providence because of Jesus! If God was not going to allow Isaac to be killed in a foreign land because of Abraham, then you can be confident that you are immortal in the will of God! Nothing can harm you; nothing can touch you as long as you are in His will!

You must be confident that God is going to feed you, take care of you, help you – you are blessed for Jesus' sake!

HOW GOD BLESSES HIS CHILDREN

"But why," say so many, "do I not see those blessings in my life?" You must understand, there is a condition to this blessing. Then Isaac sowed in that land, and received in the same year an hundredfold: and the LORD blessed him (Genesis 26:12).

Isaac could have just sat around saying, "I'm Blessed! God is going to take care of me. God will make the land bear fruit; God will bring the water; I don't have to do anything; I'm blessed! God told me He is going to take care of me." Sadly, that is what so many "believers" do today.

So how is God going to bless His covenant people? He blesses the work of our hands. The Bible says we are not to faint in our work for the Lord because God will not forget our labor of love.

God tells us not to faint because there will come those moments when we feel as though we just cannot do it anymore. We begin to think that nothing will ever change; it will never be different. We may ask, "What is the use?" And God says, "Don't faint because I am not going to forget your labor of love. I am going to bless you!"

God wants us to live in such a way that people relish our relationship with the Lord. God wants us to live in such a way that His blessings are upon our life! God's children walk victoriously through this life because Jesus is with them and will never forsake them – they are blessed!

I think lost people around us should say, "I really wish I had what you had. I really wish I had a relationship with God like you do." That is what Peter meant when he said live in such a way that men will ask you of the hope that is in you! You are to live in such a way that people are going to come and say, "You have to tell me about this relationship you have with God. I really need that. Though you do not have everything, I do see how God cares for you and how you are blessed and free. Your family is blessed; your children are blessed; you're blessed at work and blessed in your home. You have such contentment and peace and God is taking care of you."

Do you know how much money people are paying for psychiatric help? Do you know how much money is spent buying drugs to help with depression? And we as Christians, living among those helpless people, are to live in such a state of joy that they can see we are blessed!

Sure there are battles, but the fact is that God is with you! God blesses your labor; He blesses your work. God has put you into various places in life - places where other Christians will never go. God has chosen to put you there in order that you might stir up within people the fear of God. Somehow and in some way the people around you are to know that God is with you!

So do not faint. Even Isaac was treated poorly by Abimelech at first. But eventually he could see that Isaac was blessed of the Lord. Keep giving. Let people see that your contentment is in the Lord and that God is blessing you. Joyfully give away what He has given you and let people see that the Lord is your helper!

If you want to have a full life you have to learn to give every ounce of your life away. The measure with which you give is the measure used to give back to you. God has created the example of this in life – you get air; it is free. If you don't give it away you are dead! If you want to keep living, then every time you get free air you have to give it away. If you give it away, you get more! If you don't give it away, you get nothing. So spiritually – what you receive you must give away. If you give it away, you get more. If you keep it, then you get nothing else. When you begin to hoard the things that God has given because you fear losing them, then you have lost everything! When Jesus is no longer your contentment, then your life is in trouble. When your contentment is in the things that you have been given, then you will never be able to give those things away. As a result, those things will choke out your life!

Legend has it that a man was lost in the desert, just dying for a drink of water. He stumbled upon an old shack – a ramshackled, windowless, roofless, weather-beaten old shack. He looked about this place and found a little shade from the heat of the desert sun. As he glanced around he saw a pump about fifteen feet away – an old rusty water pump. He stumbled over to it, grabbed the handle, and began to pump up and down, up and down. Nothing came out.

Disappointed, he began to stagger away. It was then that he noticed, off to the side, an old jug. He looked at it, wiped away the dirt and dust, and read a message that said, "You have to prime the pump with all the water in this jug, my friend. PS: Be sure you fill the jug again before you leave."

He popped the cork out of the jug and sure enough, there was water. It was almost full of water! Suddenly, he was faced with a decision. If he drank the water, he could live. Ah, but if he poured all the water in the old rusty pump, maybe it would yield fresh, cool water from down deep in the well, all the water he wanted.

He studied the possibility of both options. What should he do, pour it into the old pump and take a chance on fresh, cool water or drink what was in the old jug and ignore its message? Should he waste all the water on the hopes of those flimsy instructions, written no telling how long ago?

Reluctantly he poured all the water into the pump. Then he grabbed the handle and began to pump - squeak, squeak, squeak. But nothing came out! He continued pumping; still nothing just - squeak, squeak, squeak. After several tries, a little bit of water began to dribble out, then a small stream, and finally it gushed! To his relief, fresh, cool water poured out of the rusty pump! Eagerly, he filled the jug and drank from it. He filled it another time and once again drank its refreshing contents.

Then he filled the jug for the next traveler. He filled it to the top, popped the cork back on, and added this little note: "Believe me, it really works. You have to give it all away before you can get anything back."

Show the world how God has blessed you. It is not the amount you have to give but how you give - the spirit in which you give!

We have been blessed in Jesus. We should ask God to help us realize the blessings we have received: the providence of God, the welfare of God, the provisions and protection of God. As with Abraham, how many times has God cared for us when we were not acting appropriately? It was for Jesus' sake. Let the nations fear God because of the blessings He wants to pour out on our lives. Oh that we would express our faith on a daily basis that this nation would fear the Lord again!

CHAPTER 6

BREAKING INTO ABUNDANCE

Is not this the fast that I have chosen? to loose the bands of wickedness, to undo the heavy burdens, and to let the oppressed go free, and that ye break every yoke? *Is it* not to deal thy bread to the hungry, and that thou bring the poor that are cast out to thy house? when thou seest the naked, that thou cover him; and that thou hide not thyself from thine own flesh? Then shall thy light break forth as the morning, and thine health shall spring forth speedily: and thy righteousness shall go before thee; the glory of the LORD shall be thy rereward. Then shalt thou call, and the LORD shall answer; thou shalt cry, and he shall say, Here I *am*. If thou take away from the midst of thee the yoke, the putting forth of the finger, and speaking vanity; And *if* thou draw out thy soul to the hungry, and satisfy the afflicted soul; then shall thy light rise in obscurity, and thy darkness *be* as the noonday: And the LORD shall guide thee continually, and satisfy thy soul in drought, and make fat thy bones: and thou shalt be like a watered garden, and like a spring of water, whose waters fail not. And *they that shall be* of thee shall build the old waste places: thou shalt raise up the foundations of many generations; and thou shalt be called, The repairer of the breach, The restorer of paths to dwell in. If thou turn away thy foot from the sabbath, *from* doing thy pleasure on my holy day; and call the sabbath a delight, the holy of the LORD, honourable; and shalt honour him, not doing thine own ways, nor finding thine own pleasure, nor speaking *thine own* words: Then shalt thou delight thyself in the LORD; and I will cause thee to ride upon the high places of the earth, and feed thee with the heritage of Jacob thy father: for the mouth of the LORD hath spoken *it*.

Isaiah 58:6-14

When did you ever see Jesus
    Hungry …
        Thirsty …
            Homeless …
                Shivering …
                Sick …
                    In prison …

Recently my wife and I were in Washington, DC for ministry. Having time to walk around, we noticed a very large population of the homeless scattered throughout the Capital area. These poor were on the streets – in full view of the multitudes who had become desensitized to the fact that suffering and needy people were lying on the park benches and underneath unsuitable shelters. What a revelation this was to me, as I considered that politicians used the poor to get elected and then, once elected, they were content to let these poor suffering souls just lie on the streets and scrape out garbage cans for food. Then it struck me, something must be done! But I reasoned to myself, "What can I do? I am just one person, without much money. I am here for just a short time, what difference could I possibly make?" But the longer I walked the city, the more the Holy Spirit assured me that these were real people feeling real pain. My wife and I had seen elderly women without proper clothing and no ability to provide food for themselves. We talked about it, and we realized that we could do something. We loaded bags with fruits, muffins, and chips and started through the streets. We didn't help everyone, but we did help everyone we could. We went downtown and handed the food out and were able to share the gospel with everyone we fed. We did not sell all we had? We did not switch careers and devote full time to street people? We simply saw a need, realized we could help, so we did!

In Isaiah 58, God is not denying Israel's enjoyment in religious disciplines. There really is a delight in the people that approach God. They enjoy this! Many enjoy going to church, singing the songs, gathering to pray. There is real enjoyment in these religious practices. We sometimes think all religious people are absolutely bored with spiritual things. But a lot of religious people actually take great delight in the ceremony. They derive pleasure in it; they love the rituals; they love the disciplines.

God says, "They seek me daily, they delight to know my ways as though they did righteousness." But God reveals that though they do some things, the weightier matters are not accomplished.

So religious Israel complains to God, "Why have we fasted and Thou seest not? Why have we afflicted our soul and thou takest no knowledge?"

God says, "Behold in the day of your fast you find pleasure, and exact all your labors. Behold, you fast for strife and debate, and to smite with the fist of wickedness: You shall not fast as you do this day, to make your voice to be heard on high."

God continues, "Do you want to know why I'm not hearing you? Why I'm not working for you? Why there aren't miracles happening for you? Why I'm not answering your prayers? You are crying out for justice and yet you are not giving justice. To get to me, you step over the needy, the poor, those who are bound, the sick, and the hurting as though they don't even exist. You are not moved with compassion. You have not shed one tear for the homeless man on the street; you pass him by while saying, 'I am fasting unto God.' "

God says, "This is the problem." [Author's paraphrase]

These religious people were selfish. They talked about righteousness as though they were righteous, but they were not. They talked about justice but refused to show justice. Their hearts were hard.

God wanted a fast that would affect the inward life, not just the outward behavior. Missing a meal does not impress God if you never weep from the fact that forty thousand people die a day because of malnutrition. One billion people in this world live in poverty. One billion people live without proper food, clothing, and shelter - one billion people! Four hundred million people suffer from malnutrition.

So what if we miss a meal when two hundred million people suffering from malnutrition are children! Christians could justify a complacent attitude by thinking, "The people are suffering from such poverty because of sin: personal sin, national sin, and probably most of the suffering are given to paganism and idolatry."

But our attitude cannot be, "Well then it serves them right!" Once upon a time, we were lost, and God did not have that attitude toward us. With all the excuses we could make for the poverty of adults, can we still overlook the fact that two hundred million children are suffering from the sins of their fathers; where is the church that's moved by this?

That calloused heart in Israel offended God. God knew that they had no idea what the results would be if He were to answer their prayers. He knew that it would cause fighting and debate and wickedness. He knew that if He were to grant their wishes, they would use it as a club to attack others.

WHAT IS THE PROBLEM

James teaches us, "… the tongue can no man tame; *it is* an unruly evil, full of deadly poison. Therewith bless we God, even the Father; and therewith curse we men, which are made after the similitude of God. Out of the same mouth proceedeth blessing and cursing. My brethren, these things ought not so to be" (James 3:8-10). Something is fundamentally wrong with a person who can praise, worship, and bless God with the mouth and at the same time curse men who are made in the image of God.

"Who is a wise man and endued with knowledge among you? Let him show out of a good conversation his works with meekness of wisdom. But if ye have bitter envying and strife in your hearts, glory not, and lie not against the truth" (James 3:13 – 1If there is bitter envy or strife in your heart, then do not deny it – admit it! Never excuse the condition of your heart by reasoning it away or justifying its condition. If something is in your heart that should not be there, then submit to the truth. Don't dodge the truth; let God expose it so your heart can be free.

This wisdom that lies against the truth is not from above but is earthly, sensual, and devilish. Where envying and strife exist, there is confusion and every evil work. This heart condition is what Isaiah tried to expose in Israel: a religious people who loved the rituals but had no wisdom. Their culture was filled with envy, strife, and every evil work.

But the wisdom that is from above is first pure, then peaceable, gentle and easy to be entreated – full of mercy and good fruits, without partiality and without hypocrisy. And the fruit of righteousness is sown in peace of them that make peace.

Righteousness is demonstrated in my efforts to live in peace with others. I must work for peace. I want to invite people to the peace that Jesus Christ is offering them – this is the ministry of reconciliation.

James said it is the lusts that rage inside us that cause all of the problems we have with people. You lust and have not. You kill and desire to have and cannot obtain: "You fight and war yet you have not because you ask not. You ask and receive not because you ask amiss that you may consume it up on your own lusts." This is the same thing Isaiah was telling Israel. Israel thought if God answered their prayers everything would be all right. They thought if God would simply do what they wanted – perform the way they wanted, deal with the people that caused them problems, then there would be peace. This is the attitude of many people today.

Both James and Isaiah reveal that the cause of all travail, aggravation, strife, and bitterness is due to the condition of the heart, not the actions of other people. And whoever denies this does not have the wisdom from above but lies against the truth.

God wants peace to abide within you. God wants your life to be truly righteous and holy. He wants you to care for people without partiality and without hypocrisy. He wants you to help others not because they are successful, educated, or wealthy; but because you want to show them the love of Christ. God does not want us to perform our acts of hospitality by thinking, "If I do this for them then somehow in the end they can do something for me."

WHY SHOULD GOD FILL US WITH HIS SPIRIT

Jesus left us in this world to do something for him – to be something – to be His witnesses! It is wrong for people to pray for God to fill them with His Spirit when they have no intention of really being a witness unto God. Many today want to be filled with the Holy Spirit for personal benefit: filled for personal wisdom, personal discernment, and personal experiences with Jesus Christ. In addition, they expect to receive personal revelations. That is absolute selfishness. God doesn't give His precious possessions so that people can simply consume them upon their own lusts. God wants you to give His gifts away. This is why many people are not receiving the baptism in the Holy Spirit. They don't understand what the purpose of being baptized in the Spirit is all about.

The fast God calls for ignites the passions within His people. David Brainerd prayed, "Oh, that I might be a flaming fire in the service of the Lord. Here I am, Lord, send me; send me to the ends of the earth... send me from all that is called earthly comfort; send me even to death itself if it be but in Thy service and to promote Thy Kingdom."

John Piper wrote this great prayer, "Lord, let me make a difference for you that is utterly disproportionate to who I am!" Can you hear the passion as he cries for something to happen through his life that is significant and so powerful that it is humanly impossible for him to have accomplished it? That's the kind of person that God fills with His Spirit.

DO YOU WONDER WHY GOD IS NOT ANSWERING YOUR PRAYERS

"Is it such a fast that I have chosen? A day for a man to afflict his soul? *Is it* to bow down his head as a bulrush, and to spread sackcloth and ashes *under him*? Wilt thou call this a fast, and an acceptable day to the LORD?" (Isaiah 58:5). But many people treat the fast as a way to manipulate God: "This is what I'm doing. God has to honor it. I fasted for three days; God has to honor it. God is obligated to answer me at the end of my three days fast." But God is not fooled by this mind-set. He determines what He will answer and man's little religious shows do not intimidate Him.

God said, "*Is* not this the fast that I have chosen? To loose the bands of wickedness, to undo the heavy burdens, and to let the oppressed go free, and that ye break every yoke? *Is it* not to deal thy bread to the hungry, and that thou bring the poor that are cast out to thy house? When thou seest the naked, that thou cover him; and that thou hide not thyself from thine own flesh." (Isaiah 58:6-7).

So when "Christians" ask, "Where are the miracles of God? Where are the answers to our prayers? I've been at the prayer meetings; I've fasted; why hasn't God heard me?" Then God is answering, "Do you know what your prayers and fasting are like to me? It is obnoxious to me" [Author's paraphrase]. God might compare your screaming at the top of your voice to a baby who cries just to get its way. Like a baby, you are throwing a temper tantrum until finally Mom and Dad give in. But guess what! The God in heaven, our Father, is not going to give in. God is saying, "All your seeking is like screaming at the top of your lungs just so I hear you. And you think that if I hear you, then I will give you what you want" [Author's paraphrase]. God is not going to succumb to this type of manipulation.

Are you wondering why you do not feel God's presence? Could His absence be due to a failure on your part to attend to the fast God has called? Have you become simply religious and no longer a true worshipper? Do you step over the poor and needy with your heart rarely affected by their plight? Do the diseased no longer grieve you; have you learned to look away? Do babies in cancer wards go unnoticed; do babies born addicted to crack cocaine rarely move your heart?

This world is broken and hurting and you are the means by which God wants to demonstrate His love! Families are suffering from suicides, disease, or divorce. Individuals are traumatized by depression, personal injuries, abuse, and betrayals. Parents will sleep in the hospital waiting room tonight. A husband will sleep on a couch in a critical care unit crying to a God he probably does not know! Where is the church in this hour?

What does God think when you get on your knees and pray, "God what is your will for my life? What would you have me to do? Would you give me a better job and more money?"

What does God think? Perhaps he would say, "You know what I want you to do today? Get some chips and cokes. Walk through a hospital waiting room. Then serve and pray for the scared and hurting! Try to relieve the wife who is being strangled with fear. Undo the burdens of the man who just got laid off from his job. Go to the schools. Teenage pregnancy is still a problem; go to these young girls and offer them hope. Go into the places where people are hurting. If they will not let you in, then find the places that will." God is asking, "How long will My church step over the hurting, lonely, and dying people in order to come worship me" [Author's paraphrase].

BEWARE! WE ARE NOT HUMANITARIANS – WE ARE AMBASSADORS

If you want to see God work for you then you need to have a heart change. God wants people to be free. He wants those that are bound in wickedness to be free. He does not want you to make the bonds of their wickedness tighter. He does not want you to kill them by the letter of the law! He wants the gospel to reach them! He put the good news into your heart that from your heart it may be used to break the bands of wickedness and heal the broken.

He wants you to draw your soul out. God does not want us simply to put water in a thirsty person's hand or put food in a hungry man's belly or to put a shirt on the back of a man that's naked. Sadly that is all modern evangelism is doing. Modern evangelism does the "humanitarian thing" but fails to bring the gospel that sets the heart free and brings peace with God into the hurting life. Do those practical things, but let your motivation be of a spiritual nature. God is not simply interested in how you can take care of the physical man, though that is very important. Your motivation is to get to the soul; to get to the heart.

Take away from the midst of you the putting forth of the finger and speaking vanity. The "putting forth of the finger" is the attitude that suggests, "That lazy bum, if he would just work he wouldn't have to live like that." Such an attitude is filled with raw, heartless accusations against those less fortunate, assuming they deserve to be in their predicaments. Are you so quick to forget where He found you? Have you forgotten how God pulled you out and put your feet on a rock, saving you?

Your mission is to love, to lay down your life, to give the good news. To give the good news you have to explain the bad. But the gospel will leave the hopeless with a hope to unlock their bondage, and that hope is the blood of Jesus Christ that sets all who believe free.

On a mission trip in the Philippines, I encountered a vile, evil man at the altar. He stood in my face. He had been wheezing all night, suffering from a severe case of asthma. He said, "I'm not a Christian. I don't want to be a Christian. I don't believe in your God. But you said your God was great. You said He could do anything. You said that He loved me. I want you to pray and I want your great God to heal me. I'm not interested in being saved."

My initial response was to put this guy in his place. How dare he treat God with such contempt. I was just about to let him know what I thought when the Holy Spirit stopped me. The Holy Spirit reminded me how often He healed people that never believed, how often He had compassion on the sick who never believed.

He told me, "I healed ten lepers and only one of them came back to thank me. Because you are offended by what he said, are you going to act in yourself and misrepresent me?" The Holy Spirit said, "Pray for him." I prayed and God healed him! I witnessed a miracle. The man threw his respirator away that night. He came back later, and he gave his heart to the Lord. God showed his love and compassion, and it reached this man's heart.

In Luke 4:18 Jesus said, "The Spirit of the Lord is upon me because he has anointed me to preach the gospel to the poor. He has sent me to heal the brokenhearted to preach deliverance to the captives and recovering of sight to the blind to set at liberty them that are bruised to preach the acceptable year of the Lord ... this day is the scripture fulfilled in your ears."

In essence Jesus was saying, "I am here to perform the fast my Father called. I have come to honor Him with that fast." And the Bible tells us that everywhere Jesus went He was moved with compassion upon the people. He had a tender heart. He was meek in His spirit, and he ministered to the people. One thing the people knew was that this man did love them, and he did great things for them.

They must have thought, "He certainly helped us. He certainly made an impact on our lives."

Jesus still wants to make an impact upon the world through our hospitality-through our giving and laying down our lives to minister to one another. It is not wrong to pray, "God, what would You have you me to do?" But it is wrong not to open your eyes to see. Maybe God would have you reach an area of your town or some unreached people group. If your eyes have been opened to see a need, then chances are that God is telling you what He wants you to do.

I have seen grown men crying as their hearts were touched by God as they fulfilled Isaiah 58. Why do so many true believers pay their own way to go on mission trips to help the hurting and relieve the oppressed if there were not such a vast reward in doing so? Many of you have tasted it. You have tasted the presence of God. You have experienced God's reality when you helped reach out into the inner city. You were blessed when you helped feed people and preach to people and minister to people.

God says, "If you serve me in the fast, I will break forth as the morning and your health shall spring forth speedily and your light shall go before you.... You will pray and I will answer. I will be with you. Your health will break forth and I will lavish you with blessings. I will satisfy your soul in drought and make fat your bones. You shall be like a watered garden, like a spring of water whose waters fail not. You shall be called the repairer of the breach, the restorer of paths to dwell in."

CHAPTER 7

HOW DO I ASK GOD TO BLESS ME?

What *doth it* profit, my brethren, though a man say he hath faith, and have not works? can faith save him? If a brother or sister be naked, and destitute of daily food, And one of you say unto them, Depart in peace, be *ye* warmed and filled; notwithstanding ye give them not those things which are needful to the body; what *doth it* profit? Even so faith, if it hath not works, is dead, being alone. Yea, a man may say, Thou hast faith, and I have works: show me thy faith without thy works, and I will show thee my faith by my works.

James 2:14 - 18

J ames said that the simplicity of our faith is expressed by ministering to those who are in need. When we involve ourselves by helping one who needs clothing or food we are displaying our faith. James brought the proof of faith into the reach of every believer when he wrote those words. He could have said, "I will show you my faith by raising the dead or walking on water." But that is not what the Holy Spirit told him to say! Rather, the Holy Spirit told James to prove the reality of faith by having an active role in relieving the distressed.

It's so easy to get geared up for a big mission trip or conference, but real Christianity is expressed in how we function in the common occurrences of everyday life. "Blessed *is* he that considereth the poor: the LORD will deliver him in time of trouble. The LORD will preserve him, and keep him alive; *and* he shall be blessed upon the earth: and thou wilt not deliver him unto the will of his enemies. The LORD will strengthen him upon the bed of languishing: thou wilt make all his bed in his sickness" (Psalm 41:1-3).

Psalms 41 reveals that God wants to break into our life with abundance. God wants to open the windows of heaven upon us. God wants us to be abundantly blessed. God wants us to prosper; He wants us to have the light of His countenance upon us!

"Blessed is the man that considereth the poor: the Lord will deliver him in time of trouble. The Lord will preserve him, and keep him alive; and he shall be blessed upon the earth ..." God will not hand him over to the will of his enemies. The Lord will strengthen him.

This is an awesome promise! The Lord says that if we consider the poor, He will bless us in a multitude of ways. Everyday God gives us the opportunity to be blessed. We are surrounded by people that are in need. Driving our cars we pass them all the time. They are holding up signs - "Will work for food." We pass them every day; they are everywhere. So how are we displaying our faith? How are we capitalizing on these promises that God has made us in Psalm 41?

The Bible teaches that when you give to the poor you are lending to the Lord, and the Lord will be no man's debtor! So when you are giving to the poor you are lending to the Lord, and God is not going to be in debt to you. He is going to pay you back. And He will pay you back abundantly.

One way that God pays back is by delivering you when you're in trouble. He delivers you because you considered the poor. The Lord preserves you and keeps you alive and blesses you upon the earth, not just in heaven! Your reward is not just in heaven, though that would be enough. God promises to bless you in this world – blessed upon the earth! What person in his right mind would refuse that? What person would say to the Lord, "I don't want your blessings?"

I want you to realize that the opportunity to show hospitality is at the heart of the gospel of Jesus Christ. When Jesus came to the world he reached out to those who were sick, to those who were cast out, and to the unaccepted. He preached the acceptable year of the Lord. Those that were bruised, He came to deliver. For those held captive, He came to set free. Jesus expressed His gospel through hospitality. He laid down his life every day to relieve the distressed. And in like manner, we are able to validate our faith by laying down our lives for one another: in our churches, in our homes and families, and for the strangers we may meet.

AVOID A FAITHLESS ATTITUDE

One of the key ingredients to being blessed by God is blessing other people - ministering to other people and assisting those who are facing distressing situations.

One great hindrance to receiving God's blessings is lack of faith. This lack of faith is expressed in the common attitude which expresses itself in ways such as, "Well I would help more if I had more means to help. I am waiting for my ship to come in. And when it comes in I fully intend to get involved in helping people that are in need and assisting others through the calamities of life. You know, when I am set up I am going to begin to do that."

So many sit around and pray, "God bless me. God make it possible for me to be able to give to others." Many say these prayers thinking they are asking God to bless them so they can help others. But how do you ask God to bless you? Do you just get down on your knees and pray, "God bless me. Bless my job. Bless my finances. Get me out of debt. Give me a promotion at work. Give me a raise! God, if you would give me a raise, if you would increase my salary, I would use that to help other people."

And so begins the barter with God. But is this really the way to ask God to bless us? Is this really what God wants to hear from our lives in order that we could be blessed? The Bible says give and it shall be given unto you, pressed down and shaken together and running over. The Bible says give unto men, and men will give back unto you, and with the measure you give you shall receive. Jesus said freely you have received freely give. Paul said if you sow sparingly you shall reap sparingly, but if you sow generously then you reap abundance. Our giving determines the quantity of our blessings.

So we have to answer this question, "How do I ask God to bless me?" Is mere giving all that is required to be blessed? Is God simply satisfied to bless me because I consider the poor by putting food on their table ... clothes on their back ... and relieving their distresses? Is that all I have to do to be blessed? Is that how I ask God to bless me?

GIVE WITH FAITH

Consider the way Jesus dealt with the Pharisees in Matthew 23:23, "Woe unto you, scribes and Pharisees, hypocrites! For ye pay tithe of mint and anise and cumin, and have omitted the weightier *matters* of the law, judgment, mercy, and faith: these ought ye to have done, and not to leave the other undone."

Jesus delivered strong rebukes against the Pharisees. These rebukes cut to the quick. So the answer to the question, "Is giving all I have to do for God to bless me?" would have to be, "No!"

The Pharisees were diligent. They tithed. They were disciplined in their religious behaviors, but Jesus rebukes them for what they were not doing. He rebukes them for omitting judgment, mercy, and faith. They appeared righteous publicly, but there was no righteousness in their heart. This shows that you can be religious, and even give, but not have faith. They tithed but not in faith. Whatever is not of faith is sin. It is so easy just to become a humanitarian. But being a humanitarian does not mean that you have faith or that you will be blessed of God.

Be careful that you do not deceive yourself by giving a homeless man a gift certificate to McDonald's and then reason, "Alright God, I considered the poor, I gave him some money and bought him a meal at McDonald's, so now Lord you have to deliver me out of my trouble." God could respond to that reasoning, "You didn't do it in faith."

HOW DOES ONE LEND TO THE LORD

The Bible says that God wants me to give with a joyful heart. God wants me to give from the understanding of why I have it to give. God has given me all things richly to enjoy. He has blessed me, and thus enabled me with the ability to help others. When the gift of His grace and mercy has been given to me, then I am excited about giving it to others. Now I can see the faith in giving. I am giving in the name of God! I am representing Him – that is how I am lending to the Lord! I am ministering to the needs of others wanting them to see the love of God and not me. I am giving in God's stead, or for God. That is how I lend to the Lord. I am not seeking glory for myself but for God. If I want anyone to see me, then I am acting in my name. At that point I am not acting in faith or for the glory of God, but for my own glory!

That is what James meant when he said he would feed the hungry and demonstrate his faith. He was letting us know that his involvement in the distress of others is because of his relationship with the Lord. James acted so others would know God - they would see Jesus and not see James, but how different it is today. It seems that the only thing people are seeing are churches helping, ministries helping, and Christians helping. Few people are seeing Jesus helping the poor through His servants.

THE MACEDONIAN EXAMPLE

God doesn't want us to give so we can barter with him. He doesn't want us to just callously help people and call this Christian hospitality – that's just humanitarian work. God wants you to make Him known to those in distress.

The Macedonians were a very poor assembly. But when they heard that the saints in Jerusalem were suffering, by the grace of God they collected gifts.

Because of their poverty they had to beg the Apostle Paul to take their gift! They literally begged Paul for the opportunity to help others! Their excitement did not come from an abundance of wealth and prosperous businesses. By the grace of God they were able to give. They were excited because they had Jesus Christ and He gave them something. They were excited about being joined to God and His kingdom. They were excited because they belonged to the Lord who would feed them, clothe them, shelter them, and protect them.

They were joyful in their God. Now they have an opportunity to help other brothers in Christ. Truly their joy was abounding in the Lord.

So Paul used the Macedonians as an example of giving. They gave by grace out of their relationship with the Lord. Their giving was not from the abundance of their wealth but out of the abundance of their joy. They gave not out of an extreme amount of wealth but out of extreme poverty! Paul says this is the way believers should give!

Don't give grudgingly. Don't give to put on a good show for Jesus, the church, and everybody else. As you purposed in your heart, that's how you give. Every man as he has purposed in his heart. Don't manipulate people attempting to get money from them. Let every man give as he purposed in his heart, understanding this great truth – that when you give sparingly you shall reap sparingly. If you give abundantly you shall reap abundantly. And God is able to make everything abound back to you so that by God's grace you are always able to do good.

DO NOT INSULT YOUR KING

So how do you ask God to bless? You give out of faith, out of joy, because you are in relationship with the King of the universe. You belong to the kingdom of heaven. God is your provider. For any believer to go around as though he has nothing to give is an insult to our King and His kingdom! Dare the Macedonians think they have no ability to help when Jesus Christ, the King of Kings and Lord of Lords, is their Redeemer and King!

Do not judge the significance of your gift. God does not use the same measurement that man uses. In the eyes of God, the million-aire who gives one hundred thousand dollars gave no more than the one who gave ten dollars from the one hundred that he made.

The widow gave her two mites; she gave everything. Nobody considered her gift as extravagant except Jesus. He said that she gave more than everybody else! Everybody else gave out of their abundance, but she gave out of her need. She gave everything.

How do you think God responded to that lady? He is going to take care of her. He will watch over her. When she's in trouble, He will deliver her. When she's languishing, He will comfort her. He will bless her.

WHY SHOULD GOD TRUST YOU WITH MORE

Now to give the final answer to the question, "How do I ask God to bless me?" Jesus said, "… as ye go, preach, saying, The kingdom of heaven is at hand. ⁸Heal the sick, cleanse the lepers, raise the dead, cast out devils: freely ye have received, freely give" (*Matthew* 10:8).

Jesus did not say freely you *will* receive. Jesus speaks as though He has already given something! According to Jesus, if you are a believer, your ship has come in! You have the means. Jesus has given you everything that is His. He now expects the believer to give it away.

When a believer approaches God with a faithless attitude saying, "Lord, things are really tight for me; I just cannot afford to help at the moment. I would like to help. I want to get involved. I want to minister to the poor and help the needy. I would love to minister to brothers in the church, and I want to show your hospitality to people. But God, right now it's really hard for me. I have nothing to give. But if you would bless me and get me out of this pit, then I promise to serve you and help others." A child of the King with no means to help! What an insult to the throne of heaven!

When you were born again God gave you something: He gave you authority, power, His spirit; He gave you His life! In Christ you have much to give. It is not the amount you give but the blessing that God puts on it! In Christ you are able. Maybe you cannot fix a meal for somebody. Because of poverty you may not even eat tonight, but you can pray; you can pick up the phone and pray for one that might be suffering. You can believe with the afflicted that God will be faithful, and you can go to them in the name of Jesus and show them His grace. That is hospitality!

When a believer says to God, "If you would help me, if you would bless me, then I would do something for you!" Does that believer have any idea how those comments may grieve the Lord?

God says, "I gave you everything. Do you know how I am grieved to hear you on your knees asking me to bless you, asking me to take care of you, telling me that if I will give you something then you would use it for My glory? I have already given you the kingdom of Heaven! You know what I want you to do? If you really mean that you will do something with the blessings that I will give you, then do something with the blessings that I have already given to you!

When I see you helping others with what I have given you, then I will always see that you have the ability to give - that your suffi- ciency is there for every situation! I will use you to bless others if I can just get what I give you through you! If it stops with you, then that is all you get, and I will eventually take that away!" [Author's paraphrase]

If you want to display the reality of your faith, you don't have to raise the dead or walk on the water. In the name of Jesus, by His grace, minister to those who are around you - those in your church and community. By that act you can display your faith. Don't give like the Pharisees but like the Macedonians, with grace and joy and faith.

PRAYER:

Lord, I ask in the powerful name of Jesus,
> To open up our eyes to the realization of what you've given us.

Lord, let us see that when we were born again we were joined to your kingdom.

You supply every need in our life through your riches in glory through Christ Jesus.

Help us God to boldly ask and believe for your blessings upon our life. We don't want to be negligent in asking you to bless and help us in every sphere of our lives. But we don't want to dishonor you and pray in ways that would insinuate that you're not taking care of us, because you are!

Sometimes in our physical life there might be things that we have to do without,
> And maybe there are some things we don't have that other people have.

But you still meet all our needs,
> And we are a blessed people;
>> Let us live in the confidence of your great faithfulness.

Teach us how to ask,
> Not only with the words we pray,
>> But by the deeds we do.

Let us give in faith!

Let us understand that you have freely given all things to us,
> And let us give these blessings away freely,
>> With no strings attached.

I desire for all to see, through my life and giving, how awesome and faithful you are to me.

CHAPTER 8

WHEN YOU NEED A TIMOTHY

Some believers, in the Body of Christ, are reserved by God for more critical moments in life. God places others in His Body who look out for the daily needs of His people. If we consider this fact we will not misjudge those who are not regularly showing the type of hospitality we want to see.

- Lee Shipp

When you need a Timothy. Think about it. Sometimes in life we need a Timothy. We need the deep strength and fortitude he can provide in the most difficult trials of life. God places many wonderful people in our lives who give daily encouragement and care. Their role in our development as men and women of God is vital. They are helpful, courteous, sensitive to our needs. But sometimes their reach is not deep enough in a great hour of struggle. It is then that we need the powerful support of a Timothy.

You see, the Timothys are not those in your life that pick you up daily, but they are those in your life that keep you from being crushed. They may not be there to fix you a meal or help you paint the kitchen or encourage you if you are just having a lousy day. But they are the ones that you must have at your side when your baby has just been rushed to the emergency room. Or as Paul testified, they are those that are there when you come to the end of your life and your faith is greatly tried! It is then that you need a Timothy!

Before I express the main point of this chapter, it is necessary to make some clarifications. Some believers, in the Body of Christ, are reserved by God for more critical moments in life. God places others in His Body who look out for the daily needs of His people. If we consider this fact we will not misjudge those who are not regularly showing the type of hospitality we want to see.

If some in the Body of Christ are not responding to your life the way you desire, it does not mean they are lacking hospitality. They could be extremely involved in very critical matters you are not aware of. They could be involved in situations where they are literally helping a believer hold on to his faith or perhaps fighting for a couple contemplating divorce. Just because they may not always be visibly encouraging everyone does not mean they lack hospitality. So be careful how you view one who seems too quiet or does not involve himself in the more common affairs of life.

NEGLECT IN THE EARLY CHURCH

"And in those days, when the number of the disciples was multiplied, there arose a murmuring of the Grecians against the Hebrews because their widows were neglected in the daily ministration. Then the twelve called the multitude of the disciples *unto them*, and said, "It is not reason that we should leave the word of God, and serve tables" (Acts 6:1-2).

Understand that there was a daily administration of meeting needs. Every day, widows would come for their needs to be met from the provisions that were in the church. Oftentimes the Gentiles were being overlooked and the Hebrews were given preferential treatment. The neglected widows did not gripe, complain, and leave the church. They didn't develop a negative attitude reasoning within, "I'm not talking to those people anymore because they neglected me."

The widows brought their concern to the proper authority, the apostles. Recognizing the problem, the apostles then called the church together explaining how this matter should be handled.

Though there was a problem - widows in the church were being neglected - the apostles refused to allow this issue to take them from their appointed tasks, "It is not reason that we should leave the word of God, and serve tables."

Now such a response may sound rather harsh. I am sure that many in the church could misjudge the apostles' intentions and consider them inhospitable. One may even think that the apostles are demeaning the responsibility of those who will be appointed to this task. But to the contrary, the apostles do not think they are too important to do such a lowly task. For them to think their prestige or high reputation is above waiting tables would spurn the teachings of Jesus. Jesus' apostles were not above doing ordinary and common duties; they knew how to wash feet! Jesus taught them that the true servant is not the person who puts himself above people, but a true servant is willing to put himself in a lower position; he does not seek to be served, but to serve. Rest assured this servant's spirit is in the heart of the apostles, and they do not regard themselves as being better than others, nor do they consider the task of meeting the daily needs to be beneath them.

PETER'S WISE DECISION

What the apostles are doing in this situation is distributing important tasks among the Body of Christ. The apostles recognized they could not do everything. If they were to sit at these tables every day, monitoring that the widows were treated fairly, then they would have to neglect the responsibilities that God gave them, "...[to]... give ourselves continually to prayer, and to the ministry of the word."

That people receive food is important, but the apostles knew that their calling was to ensure that the church received spiritual food; that believers were being fed and nurtured in the things of God.

The daily ministration of needs to the widows was a beautiful display of hospitality by the church. The apostles could have given themselves to the task and become regarded as deeply "caring men." But they saw this task as a distraction, drawing them away from praying and studying God's word. If they allowed this ministration to draw them from their calling, in the long run, no one would be hospitable. When it comes time to minister to the body of Christ, when it comes time to watch over the church, when it comes time to help believers grow and mature in the Lord - to share Scripture; they are not going to be able to do it because they have spent too much time waiting tables.

I find I have enough upon me to crush me unless heaven sustains me. My brother and the elders do for me what the elders in the wilderness church did for Moses, else should I utterly faint; but the more difficult cases, and the general leadership, make up a burden which none can carry unless the Lord gives strength. ... Beside all this, there cometh upon me the care of many another church, and of all sorts of works for our Lord. There, you do not know all, but you may guess; if you love me, if you love my Master, I implore you, pray for me. A good old man prayed ... that I might always be delivered from the bleating of the sheep. I did not understand what he meant; but I know now, when hour by hour all sorts of petitions, complaints, bemoanings, and hard questions come to me. The bleating of the sheep is not the most helpful sound in the world, especially when I am trying to get the food ready for the thousands here, there, and everywhere, who look for it to come to them regularly, week by week. Sometimes, I become so perplexed that I sink in heart, and dream that it were better for me never to have been born than to have been called to bear all this multitude upon my heart. Especially do I feel this when I cannot help the people who come to me, and yet they expect that I should do impossibilities. [Spurgeon, *Only a Prayer Meeting,* pp. 151-152.]

So understand that the apostles were not demeaning this task and giving it to lesser men. Notice what the apostles said was required to do this job, "... look ye out among you seven men of honest report, full of the Holy Ghost and wisdom, whom we may appoint over this business." This job could not be trusted to just anybody, not even to a skilled business manager if he lacked the above qualifications.

SPIRITUAL MEN ARE NEEDED

What is needed are men of honest report, full of the Holy Ghost and wisdom. The apostles were saying that the men that do this work for the church have to be spiritual! Though the apostles are given to prayer and studying the Word, their calling is not the only spiritual one in the church. Whatever is done in the church, if it is to be done properly to the glory of God, requires the leadership of the Holy Ghost. So all work in the church is spiritual whatever that task may be.

Now some people within the church have the responsibility of deep prayer, studying God's Word, and being prepared and ready to feed the people of God in a consistent and a balanced way. Other people within the church are set apart to do physical jobs: managing the affairs of the church, caring for the physical needs of the people, and so forth. People from within the Body have to rise up and make sure the sick are being taken care of, that the hungry are being fed, and that those who suffer lack are being supplied.

If the pastor tried to do everything, then eventually nothing would be done. The pastor would also be robbing believers of the enjoyment of serving God and His people. So understand there is a daily need. The apostles were letting the church know: we are not going to be here every day; we are not going to be at these tables; you are not going to see us on a regular and consistent basis when you come to have your physical needs met. Instead you will see other men, full of the Holy Ghost and wisdom, taking care of you. They are the ones you are going to see every day, not us. They are the ones that will be meeting your physical needs, not us.

THE HOLY SPIRIT IS NECESSARY

Here is one reason the men assigned to daily tasks had to be filled with the Holy Ghost. If they were not governed by the Holy Spirit they could begin to usurp the role of the minister and the apostles. They would become arrogant, saying to the people, "You see who takes care of you. You see who meets with you every day. Do you see Peter here every day? Do you see John caring about your needs?

"No, you don't see them here! You see us. We are the ones here every day; we are the ones that really care about you. Those Apostles really don't care about you; if they did, they would be here for you!"

A man that lacked the Holy Ghost and wisdom would begin to take that credit to himself and lift himself up in pride above the others. The Holy Spirit is required to keep his servants humble so the church functions properly.

THE SEVEN MEN WERE AN EXTENSION OF THE APOSTLES

"... and when they had prayed, they laid *their* hands on them. And the word of God increased; and the number of the disciples multiplied in Jerusalem greatly ..." (Acts 6:6-7).

The apostles are making a public commendation of these men. The church selected seven men believed to be filled with the Holy Ghost - men of wisdom and integrity. By laying hands upon these men, the apostles were in agreement with the decision. Through prayer the seven men were set apart in the church to care for the widows' needs.

It is vital that we understand the purpose of the apostles' laying their hands on these seven men. The significance of the laying on of hands, though it carries many spiritual truths, certainly was a demonstration of this important function: These seven men became an extension of the apostles. In other words, the apostles were saying, "These seven men are not taking care of your needs instead of us, but rather we are taking care of your needs through them. We believe that your needs are important. We believe that you should be taken care of physically. Because we are not allowed to do everything, we are agreeing that these men are qualified to serve you. We are laying our hands upon them so you will always see that through these men, we are serving you!"

Today this ministry is still occurring. Men from the church visit the sick in hospitals. They are there for the pastor; they are an extension of the pastor's ministry. As a pastor, I will call someone and tell them I need help, "A brother is in the hospital. I need you to go visit him for me. Would you please go pray for him?" So the servant goes and visits the sick brother. They don't go in that room and say, "I'm here because Pastor Lee does not care about you. If he cared he would be here instead of me." That servant would be usurping my position and taking prideful opportunities to lift himself above the pastor.

If the definition of being careless is that you do not go visit in the hospital, then few people ever care! And what about the people that you will never get to help or visit? Is it because you do not care? No! It is because you cannot do everything! That is why Jesus has a body. Someone in the body will be there to help! It doesn't always have to be you! Not being there for someone in need does not mean you don't care; it simply means that Jesus wanted to use someone else that time!

When believers are ministering in the power of the Holy Ghost they minister on behalf of the church. They are not there with an "I" mentality. "I am here because I care about you. I wanted to see you. I wanted to help you. I wanted to check on you." Rather, they let the needy know, "The church cares about you. The pastor wants to know how you're doing. He asked me to come because he is indisposed at the moment, but he cares about you. That is why I am here in his place. We have you on the prayer line; we are all praying for you.

I commend the attitude of the church in Acts 6. We do not find any of these widows saying, "Well I think it is pitiful that Peter and John are not here. They should at least be here once a week, or they should be here three times a week, or they should at least come once a month." You don't hear any of that. There was a problem; the leaders gave the solution; and the people accepted it. Do you know why? It was too early in the game for people to become superstars. These all recognized the answer - Jesus Christ! It is Jesus Christ filling His people with the Holy Spirit and then living through them!

I don't have to have a pastor pray for me, but I do need a believer full of the Holy Ghost to pray for me. That's what I need. I don't have to have a pastor counsel me, but I do need a believer full of wisdom. So the early church was content because their needs would be cared for by men full of the Holy Ghost.

THE CHURCH IS GROWING

As a result of Peter's leadership, we find, "… the word of God increased; and the number of the disciples multiplied in Jerusalem greatly…." Disciples are increasing because more believers are given the opportunity to spread the word. Peter can only be at one place at a time. Now, because of Peter's decision, there are seven other men recognized within the church as ministers.

Stephen goes on to become a very mighty preacher of the gospel of Jesus Christ. Though his ministry was cut short (they stoned him to death), his boldness made a profound impact upon the apostle Paul.

The Bible tells us Stephen was full of faith and power. Stephen has come to a place where he confidently exercises his faith. Could it be that Stephen's devotion to Jesus was motivated by the recognition of the church? The church commended his walk with God saying something to this effect, "The apostles told us to set apart seven men who could care for our needs. These have to be godly men, full the Holy Ghost and full of wisdom. Stephen, we believe you're one of those men." How do you think that affected him? I think he was overjoyed. I think he was excited and thankful to God that people could witness his walk with Jesus Christ.

The Bible says to live in such a way that the church can see how God is using you. Live in such a way that the church can see your growth and the gifts God has placed in your life. As with Stephen, how wonderful is it when the recognition comes? For Stephen it must have been one of the greatest days of his life!

Surely Stephen's faith was greater because of this recognition, "The church has seen Christ in me and witnessed the fact that I am full of the Holy Ghost. The church has witnessed the wisdom that God has given me and the integrity that I have in Jesus Christ. The apostles affirmed it!"

Stephen teaches us that no one becomes a vessel of real spiritual significance unless he start in the area of hospitality. How can God use a person greatly who does not express his love and faith by refreshing the Saints? You are going to find that the most valuable people in the Body of Christ, if I may use that qualification, are the ones concerned that the people of God make it. They are not trying to break the spirits of people, nor do they shut the gates of heaven to those that are striving to enter.

The most valuable ministers in the Body of Jesus Christ are the ones that are cheering people on, encouraging them to continue when it feels as though their faith is failing. They want believers to continue because that's what Jesus Christ wants for all His people.

Peter's leadership caused the early church to recognize that the Body of Christ is big, and the more people that are involved in serving, exercising their gifts, and doing the most common tasks will be the ones who go on to do some of the greatest things for Jesus.

You have to start somewhere. God is not going to let your first crusade be in a football stadium filled with eighty thousand people. You start by sharing the Word with your family and friends. Perhaps hold Bible studies in your office or home. Eventually your hospitality will make way for greater open doors!

FOR THE CRITICAL MOMENTS OF LIFE

Now I want to share what is really burdening my heart. Let's look closely at the situation: *When You Need a Timothy.* Believers, we must be careful about comparing ourselves with one another and falsely judging how hospitable another brother in Christ may be, for God has various assignments for us. As with the apostles, there may be some who do not attend to your daily needs. But when deeper and more critical events occur then you will find their service and love to be extreme and abundant! "The Lord give mercy unto the house of Onesiphorus; for he oft refreshed me, and was not ashamed of my chain...." (2 Timothy 1:16).

Onesiphorus is a man who consistently refreshed Paul both spiritually and physically: he encouraged Paul, stood with Paul, was a friend to Paul, and understood Paul. He was somebody Paul was comfortable with. Onesiphorus was not ashamed of Paul's imprisonments; he was not embarrassed because of Paul's persecutions. "... when he was in Rome, he sought me out very diligently, and found *me*. The Lord grant unto him that he may find mercy of the Lord in that day: and in how many things he ministered unto me at Ephesus, thou knowest very well." Onesiphorus is a great man. His hospitality to Paul was nothing short of wonderful and fabulous.

In Paul's letter to Timothy, we find Paul facing one of the greatest trials in his life. He is about to die. I want you to notice who

Paul asks for: "Do thy diligence to come shortly unto me ... Do thy diligence to come before winter" (2 Timothy 4:9, 21). Do you see Paul's heart? Surely you remember what he said about Timothy, "I have no other person in my life like Timothy." So Paul says, "I have come to the end of my life. I have finished my race. Now, at the end, this is what I need, this is who I need - I need you. I need you Timothy! At the end of my life I want you to be here!"

Paul does not ask for Timothy to stop by Ephesus and pick up Onesiphorus, though Onesiphorus was there for Paul - helping and comforting him. What Paul needs right now is Timothy's hospitality.

The caution we must exercise when judging another's hospitality and gifts, must rest on the fact that we have no idea how some, who rarely minister into our lives, are bearing such a load in rescuing other brothers whose faith may be failing! God might be preparing them to be the very means through which we receive strength in our most critical hour.

So do not accuse some in the Body of Christ for not caring. As the apostles, they may have very demanding tasks that God will not release them from in order to wait on tables. So many things happen in the Body of Christ. Many times we walk in church and wonderful brothers and sisters are lavishing us with hospitality. They are the Stephens and Onesiphorus'! They are refreshing! They are the ones we want to go around with or have lunch with – just wonderful people: always helping, always hospitable, always looking for encouraging things to do.

The Body of Christ desperately needs these most gifted and Spirit-filled believers who faithfully build you up in the Lord. But then there are others. When big things come: When your unwedded daughter is pregnant and she is not talking or listening, who are you going to call then? If you find that your spouse is having an affair, who do you call then? If you gambled all your money away and you do not know how to pay your house note, who are you going to talk with then? If you are a single mom whose life is being prematurely taken and you must make sure your baby will be cared for, who are you going to call? When you have been tried and your faith has become weak and you need something solid, who are you going to call then? It is at that point you need Timothy!

That is when people who were not there at the daily ministrations of your life come through – they are there when your faith is about to fail! When you say, "I can't take another step; I can't face another day; I cannot go on any more!" Then here comes that Timothy! When the catastrophes of life strike, when the storms and winds blow against you, when it seems inevitable that your house is going to fall and you are so scared, it is then a Timothy comes into your life and establishes you until the storm passes, and your house is left standing.

Paul could say, "A lot of people ministered to my life; many people blessed me; numbers of people helped me; there have been many great friends along the way. But Timothy, at the end of my life, I need you." I need you to affirm to me the care of the churches. I need you to pick up John Mark and bring him; he is profitable. I need to know that the churches are in your hands because your hands are able; your heart is willing, and your faith is certain.

Sometimes that is what people need. They need that shoulder to cry on, not just somebody to pat them on the back saying, "It's going to be okay." Even though we all need that daily encouragement, there are moments in life when that pat on the back is not going to get us through the day. We need something more from God, and the Timothy's will bring the strength we need: a person who cares, a person we can talk to, a person who can bind up our wounds.

If you are in Christ and fellowship in His body, I guarantee you that Timothy will be there when the need is expressed among the members of Christ. It is wonderful for so many of us who have found our Timothys! What a blessing it is to know that God has established someone in our life for those critical moments. It is also wonderful that God has put within the Church the people that are there to take care of our daily needs: the phone call that encourages us and the prayers offered on our behalf. It is the Spirit, and it is the Body of Christ – this is the most beautiful thing that anyone can ever be a part of!

CHAPTER 9

REBEKAH'S HOSPITALITY

And I came this day unto the well, and said, O Lord God of my master Abraham if now thou do prosper my way which I go: Behold, I stand by the well of water; and it shall come to pass, that when the virgin cometh forth to draw *water*, and I say to her, Give me, I pray thee, a little water of thy pitcher to drink; And she say to me, Both drink thou, and I will also draw for thy camels: *let* the same *be* the woman whom the LORD hath appointed out for my master's son. And before I had done speaking in mine heart, behold, Rebekah came forth with her pitcher on her shoulder; and she went down unto the well, and drew *water*: and I said unto her, Let me drink, I pray thee. And she made haste, and let down her pitcher from her *shoulder*, and said, Drink, and I will give thy camels drink also: so I drank, and she made the camels drink also (Genesis 24:42-46).

B ecause of his covenant with the Lord and the future that God has assured him, Abraham is very careful to find the proper bride for his son Isaac. Abraham instructs his most trusted servant to travel to Mesopotamia and return with a wife for Isaac.

The responsibility upon the servant is great. Because of the covenant, the servant must find the woman of God's choice. Isaac's wife must be a person that will honor God and this covenant. Finding the right wife for Isaac is a tremendous responsibility. Concerned that he may not find a woman in Mesopotamia to return to Isaac, the servant asks Abraham for advice.

Abraham explains, "God brought me out of the house of my fathers into this land. If the woman you find will not come with you then you come home. Do not bring Isaac to meet her. I free you from the charge that I'm giving you. If she will not come with you, you are not responsible anymore."

As the servant is approaching Mesopotamia, he begins to pray, seeking the Lord's assistance. He can't pick just anybody. Imagine the weight on this servant; he loves Abraham and Isaac. He is sent to another country to find a wife for his friend! It is hard enough for people to find a spouse on their own. But here is a man sent to strangers to find, in a moment, the woman who would become betrothed to his friend – he has to join two people together who have never seen each other. What a responsibility!

Once Abraham dies, this man is going to be Isaac's servant. Think about that! If he doesn't come back with the right woman, then he will have to live with that couple the rest of his life! So, wise man that he is, he prays! God answers his prayer. He laid out a condition before God and God responds.

In that day, people didn't travel alone. Rebekah would go back with him. She would bring her maid. The servant had to have provisions to bring them back to the land. He also traveled with gifts: gold, silver, and such to honor the family. Food must also be provided for the animals. Rebecca would be traveling with more than one camel. There would be a caravan.

GOD'S BEAUTIFUL PICTURE

What a beautiful picture God is painting. This story portrays how the Holy Spirit has come to receive a bride for the Son of God. The Holy Spirit is very careful in the selection of Jesus' bride. Jesus will receive His bride unto Himself; He will take his bride to be with him in heaven. His bride will abide in His Father's house.

Receiving a bride for Isaac is the shadowing of the great event we call the Rapture of the Church. Rebekah must come to the Promised Land. Isaac cannot go there. The journey that Rebekah is about to take demands faith! Rebekah is chosen to be the wife of a man she's never seen.

As the servant explains to Rebekah's family how God had blessed his trip, they can see the hand of God at work. But they reason to the servant to let her stay a little while longer at home. The servant says, "No! We need to go immediately. We cannot stay nor tarry. The Lord has given me favor. If this is the work of God then let me take her now and let her be wed to Isaac."

They agreed, but said, "We need to ask her if this is what she wants." It is explained to Rebekah that this man wants to take her to a far country to marry his master's son. She is told that it is required that she leave immediately.

Rebekah said, "I will go!" Rebekah's faith is amazing! Rebekah is saying, "I will go to this one I've never seen. I will become his bride. I will leave my family, my kindred, not knowing when I will ever see them again. I will do this because it is in my heart to do so. My heart wants to go!" She didn't have to do it. But she joined the caravan and went with Isaac's servant to the land of Canaan.

REBEKAH MEETS ISAAC

Now this was no easy journey. There were many perils along the way: the heat of the desert, the dangers of traveling, exposure when sleeping out in blankets and tents. There were trials and tests. Yet all the trials served as her preparation for the moment she would meet Isaac.

Finally they arrive at their destination. Isaac is waiting. He lifts up his eyes, and he sees the camels. Rebekah lifts up her eyes, and when she sees Isaac, she gets off the camel - now she does not know this man is Isaac! But she is excited about this man she sees. She asks the servant who he is. The servant tells her it's his master.

Well how did she know this was Isaac? Because just as the Holy Spirit is preparing the church, the servant has been preparing Rebekah. All along the trip he has been telling her about Isaac. Just as the Holy Spirit tells us about Jesus, the servant has so filled Rebecca's heart with the knowledge of Isaac that she knows him before she ever sees him. Likewise with us – the Holy Spirit fills our heart with Jesus, and oh the wonderful day when we see Him for the first time – how we will leap and run to be near him!

Rebekah is very beautiful. Isaac is very handsome. But there is something more than physical attraction going on here. God is doing something. Isaac is walking through the fields. He sees the camels come. Rebekah lights off the camel and the two meet.

Isaac brings her into Sara's tent and Rebekah becomes his wife. He loves her! This is a beautiful picture of the church's betrothal to Jesus Christ

The Holy Spirit has come seeking a bride for the Father's Son. He goes through the world asking, "Will you go with me?" Our hearts respond, "We've never seen Him. We've never been to that country." And yet our hearts say, "Yes! We want to go!"

When we begin to approach the Father's house we are going to see His Son. Rebecca had to go through many trials to get her to that place where Isaac lived, but it was worth it all when she saw Isaac!

Someday we are going to see the Son: the one that we love. Just as Rebekah had to go through many trials to get to that place in Canaan where her groom was waiting, so we too must pass through many trials as we travel on our journey to meet our beloved Savior! So, we continue to go on no matter how difficult the journey because we believe His love and presence will be worth every sacrifice. He is going to love and cherish us and take us unto Himself, and we will be joined to Him forever.

What a beautiful picture this is! In this union between Isaac and Rebekah, Isaac was faithful to Rebekah all of his life. In a day when men had many wives and concubines, Rebekah was his only wife and his only love. Isaac loved Rebekah and was faithful to her all the days of his life. This is a description of Jesus' love for us! We are the "apple of His eye."

Now I must bring out a very powerful truth from the story. How did the servant know whom to choose? Why was his prayer to God such as it was?

Rebecca represents the church; the servant represents the Holy Spirit receiving the Lord's bride. The servant prayed, "Lord, when I get to the well and I say to the woman who comes, 'Would you give me some water to drink out of your pitcher?' Lord, let her be the one!"

This is not a simple matter or some prayer thrown into the air. The Holy Spirit is moving him in this prayer. Notice what the Holy Spirit tells us in Matthew 24.

> Who then is a faithful and wise servant, whom his lord hath made ruler over his household, to give them meat in due season? Blessed *is* that servant, whom his lord when he cometh shall find so doing. Verily I say unto you, That he shall make him ruler over all his goods. But and if that evil servant shall say in his heart, My lord delayeth his coming; And shall begin to smite *his* fellowservants, and to eat and drink with the drunken; The lord of that servant shall come in a day when he looketh not for *him*, and in an hour that he is not aware of, And shall cut him asunder, and appoint *him* his portion with the hypocrites: there shall be weeping and gnashing of teeth (Matthew 24:45-51).

This scripture correlates with Isaac and Rebekah's story. So here's the question: Who is faithful and wise that Jesus wants to come for? This is the same question the servant of Abraham is asking. Who is it that should be betrothed to Isaac? Who is the woman with wisdom? Who is the woman that is godly? Who is the woman that is faithful? Jesus is telling us that He is coming to receive a people faithful and wise.

WHAT IS A HYPOCRITE

Jesus compares faithfulness with people that are involved, not just doing anything but doing the Father's will. Now I want this to be clear: Everyone who is born again will be raptured. Our righteousness and holiness is in the blood of Jesus Christ alone! He is our faithfulness, and He has fulfilled the law of God on our behalf. When Jesus died, He nailed to His cross everything that would hinder us from coming to God, and He fulfilled, on our behalf, what we could never fulfill. Just as by Adam's transgression many were made sinners, so by the obedience of one - the Lord Jesus Christ - all shall many be made righteous! That must be clear. We have to understand that faithfulness has to do with our faith in the work of Jesus on the cross and not our performance. Now, that being said, James tells us (as I will explain in a moment) that if our faith in Jesus is alive, then it will produce a life in us that proves that faith! Obviously, there are many in the church who are not sincere in their faith. Though they are busy and religious, they have no personal relationship with Jesus; their hearts are not affected by His soon return!

Jesus said that at an unexpected time, He would come! I don't believe many people today are expecting Jesus Christ to come. Very little is taught or preached on the subject. There's very little excitement and anticipation within the people that are about to meet Jesus Christ. Yet, as the servant made clear to Rebekah's family, even so the Holy Spirit is saying, "We can't wait. We cannot tarry. We must be leaving soon!"

Let me paraphrase Jesus' words as he warns, "When I come many of you will be doing things in my house, doing things in my name, but I'm not bringing hypocrites home with me."

The hypocrites in this particular portion of Scripture are those servants, each who said in his **heart**, "My Lord delays His coming." Paul said that we are to long for, to look for, and to love the appearing of the Lord Jesus Christ

How many of you in your heart are saying, "Jesus is coming soon. Jesus is really coming soon!" Or perhaps your heart is saying, "Jesus is not going to come today; Jesus will not come this month; Jesus will not come this year. I am going to get around to catching up on my tithes and getting right with people; I am going to get around to dealing with my heart and my bitterness and my unforgiveness; I am going to get around to doing that, but I have time! If that is your attitude, then you are saying in your heart that Jesus is delaying his coming. Jesus calls that attitude the response of an evil servant! If you really knew he was coming tonight, you would not put off these things!

Hypocrites are those who smite their fellow servants. They wound the people who are serving the same Lord - the same King. People who smite others who are joined together with them in the yoke of Christ are hypocrites!

You will find flaws in the most mature of God's servants, characteristics that may offend you. But the servants of Jesus Christ do not smite one another. The servants of Jesus Christ do not attack one another.

Jesus also described the hypocrite as one who drinks with the drunken. When you live with the world, drink with the world, and party with the world; you don't really expect the coming of Jesus Christ. Jesus made it clear that He will not bring hypocrites home with Him. God will not bring the evil servant home with Him. Jesus says the faithful will go with Him. And He equates faithfulness with those that are doing His will. They are not smiting fellow servants. Neither are the faithful drunk with the world's pleasures.

It is not works that save us. Nor is our faithfulness a means for personal boasting – our salvation comes only by the grace of God. Saving faith produces a new life! Not a perfect life but a perfect heart. A heart that smites hypocrisy! The born again will fight hypocrisy in their lives.

A man can say he has faith. But true faith will be faithful! Faithfulness can be measured; faith can be measured, "What doth it profit, my brethren, though a man say he hath faith, and have not works? Can faith save him? If a brother or sister be naked, and destitute of daily food, And one of you say unto them, Depart in peace, be ye warmed and filled; notwithstanding ye give them not those things which are needful to the body; what doth it profit? Even so faith, if it hath not works, is dead, being alone. Yea, a man may say, Thou hast faith, and I have works: show me thy faith without thy works, and I will show thee my faith by my works" (James 2:14 – 18).

It is wonderful that faithfulness here and in Matthew 24 has to do with how we treat one another.

SATAN IS A TERRORIST

Nothing destroys a church like gossip. I have pastored for over twenty-five years. I've seen all kinds of behaviors and attacks. I have seen moral failure. I have seen sin that is unbelievable. But nothing has hurt the church like gossip and slander. The little things that have occurred have caused more problems than major issues: small talk about this person - little jabs here and there. Little things like discontented people getting on the phones trying to find somebody in the church who will listen to their discontent: somebody upset them, somebody offended them, and they talk to somebody else about what somebody else did – this is the work of the enemy.

That's not the character of God, but people do it! If I really believe that Jesus Christ is coming and you come wanting to talk to me about so-and-so – forget it! I will not allow it!

This is what the devil does: he comes along and says, "Hey Tim, let me tell you about so and so …."

And Tim says, "That is sin! I will not be a part of it."

So Satan leaves Tim and says to Jimmy, "Hey let me tell you what so and so did."

Jimmy says, "Tell me."

And the devil loves it for he has one that he can use and seduce!

Satan begins to feed and distract Jimmy. And Satan keeps working through those hypocrites, going to person after person seeking whom he may devour! Do you know what that Devil is doing? He is building strongholds. He's not a foolish enemy. He is not dumb. When he attacks he believes he can overthrow.

Before he attacks, as any good general would do, he makes sure the flanks are in place. He makes sure he's got people on the front-line. He makes sure he's got people in the back for those that might retreat; he's preparing his strongholds. And how does he do it? He goes from one person to another trying to find someone that will listen to his complaints and murmurings, someone who will pick up the phone and complain with him about the church. He searches for someone who will talk with him about so-and-so in the church. He searches for someone who will let him tell them how others have treated him wrongly.

And whoever joins him becomes a stronghold – they serve as Satan's stronghold!

He begins to pull at that person. When the strongholds are built throughout the lives of those in the congregation, when he has successfully made many people discontent, when he has caused slandering and gossiping among church members, and when nobody was really noticing and most thought everything was fine, all of a sudden – Boom: he fights, he hits, he attacks! And most of the congregation is in shock and confusion wondering, "What is going on here?"

Satan waits for the appropriate time. He is a terrorist and strikes to kill all and destroy by the elements of cowardice and deception.

I do not want to be an evil servant. I do not want to be doing and watching things that would embarrass me at the coming of the Lord. I want to be faithful, not harmful. I do not want to be a stronghold for Satan.

WHAT IS FAITHFULNESS

Jesus did not say that He was coming back for those that preached 240 times in 2009 or for those that led 35 people to Christ. Faithfulness to God is evident in those who have Christ living in them. They express the life of Jesus in everyday life: When they see one in need – they help! When they see somebody hungry – they feed them. They are tender, compassionate, gentle, patient, laboring in love, and waiting for Jesus.

No, the works do not save – it is not necessarily the busy that are faithful. Matthew 7 says that not everyone that says Lord, Lord shall enter the kingdom of heaven. And many will say to Jesus, look what we have done in your name. We have cast out devils, prophesied, and worked miracles. But Jesus will say to them, "…I never knew you!" God wants us to be Christ-like for the sake of Christ. Faithfulness is overcoming hypocrisy: When I realize that my heart is not His heart, and my thoughts are not His thoughts, I then humbly fall and admit, "No! My heart is not perfect in every regard; my thoughts are not absolutely clean. Make me like You. Give me your heart."

REBEKAH'S SIMPLE ACT WAS THE KEY TO HER FUTURE

The servant said, "Lord, help me find the proper wife for Isaac. Let her be the one who gives me water." It is not coincidence that James demonstrated living faith by the action of giving water to the thirsty. We find back in Genesis 24 the same action of faith. Rebekah not only gave the servant her pitcher of water, but she watered every animal! Rebekah drew water out of the well for a caravan of camels. I have no idea how much water camels drink, but I would imagine that it was a difficult task. And the whole time the servant is thinking, "That is the wife of a patriarch – she is hospitable!"

Little did she know that by this simple act of godliness and common courtesy, she was giving her résumé to the man who could give her a future with the man of her dreams, ***all because she gave the water!***

Let your faith be alive with the expectancy of the coming of Jesus Christ. I'm moved to tell people about the Lord. I'm moved to forgive. I'm moved to study because Jesus is coming. Like Rebekah I want to go today! I do not want to be here for ten more days. I want to see Him, to be with Him.

John Wesley said,
Do all the good you can …
    By all the means you can …
        In all the ways you can …
            In all the places you can …
                At all the times you can …
                    To all the people you can …
                        As long as you ever can!

CHAPTER 10

ENCOURAGEMENT

"Now our Lord Jesus Christ himself, and God, even our Father, which hath loved us, and hath given *us* everlasting consolation and good hope through grace, Comfort your hearts, and stablish you in every good word and work" (2 Thessalonians 2:16 – 17).

When thinking about God, many rarely consider Him in the role of an encourager. But God has always demonstrated that His special joy and desire is pouring courage into somebody who needs it!

Paul prays that believers will experience the love of God. Being loved by God brings an everlasting comfort and good hope which establishes our faith and gives our hearts peace. The believer's faith should be undisturbed as he experiences the reality that God has loved him with an everlasting love. God's love never fails nor wavers: it hopes all things, believes all things, and endures all things.

There are times when I enjoy the comfort of a group of Christians or enjoy the comfort and good hope that a godly counselor may provide. Comforting is the love I receive from the Body of Christ. It is wonderful to be loved and helped by fellow believers, but these are not the things that comfort and stablish my life. My ultimate comfort and security comes from the love and comfort that God alone provides. In His love I cannot be moved; He has established me!

In John 14 Jesus calls the Holy Spirit the Comforter. Comforter is also translated Encourager. Considering all the Holy Spirit will do in the earth, it is wonderful that the Lord Jesus calls the Holy Spirit the Encourager! Jesus is careful to assure believers that the one coming in His name, to take up residency within our lives, will be our strength and power! God values this position of comforting men.

It is important that Jesus chose this title to describe the Holy Spirit's functioning role among the redeemed. What courage would it give if the one coming had no power to help us? What good would the Comforter be if He possessed no wisdom by which to lead us? What good would the Comforter be if He did not have the patience and love to perfect that which concerns us? What good would this Comforter be if He could not work everything together for the good of those who love God?

But Jesus said it was expedient that He go away in order for the Comforter to come. Jesus further explained that when the Comforter comes you will find out that He is Wisdom and Power and Love and Perfection and so much more! He will give you power when you are weak. He will give you wisdom when you don't know what to do. He will lead you when you have lost your way. He will lift you up when you have been knocked down. He will put joy in your spirit when you are overcome with depression. He knows the enemy you will fight tomorrow. He knows what is required to meet and defeat that enemy. He prepares you not simply to fight, but to win!

The dictionary defines encouragement as the act of inspiring others with renewed courage, renewed spirit, or renewed hope. In the New Testament encouragement is *parakalein*. This term comes from two Greek words: *para*, meaning "alongside of," and *kaleo*, meaning "to call." When others come alongside us during difficult times to give us renewed courage, a renewed spirit, renewed hope – that's encouragement.

The Holy Spirit has come to be our lifelong partner and help! He will never abandon or leave us. In the times of my life when I have sinned, the Holy Spirit was the first one to come to me: ministering conviction, repentance, and the blood of Jesus. He has never failed me.

The ministry of encouragement stands near the top of God's priority list. The Holy Spirit often encourages us through His Word. When passing through a particular trial we open the Bible and suddenly the Holy Spirit begins to speak out of His Word. It becomes alive to us. He has just encouraged us. He has brought something to our heart. There are many ways the Holy Spirit can encourage us; He can encourage through a song or in the solitude of the prayer closet. He encourages by giving us gifts and abilities. He gives us power over all the enemy and authority to demonstrate the kingdom of heaven in any given situation.

Often the Holy Spirit will use members in His body to provide the needed comfort; but we recognize that it is God doing the comforting through His people.

William Barclay says,

Again and again we find the Parakalein is the word of the rallying-call; it is the word used of the speeches of leaders and of soldiers who urge each other on. It is the word used of words which send fearful and timorous and hesitant soldiers and sailors courageously into battle. A Parakletos is therefore an Encourager, one who puts courage into the fainthearted, one who nerves the feeble arm for fight, one who makes a very ordinary man cope gallantly with a perilous and a dangerous situation ... the word, Parakalein is the word for exhorting [others] to noble deeds and high thoughts; it is especially the word of courage before battle. Life is always calling us into battle, and the one who makes us able to stand up to the opposing forces, to cope with life and to conquer life is the Parakletos, the Holy Spirit, who is none other than the presence and power of the risen Christ.

FRUSTRATING SATAN

We cannot stand against Satan without the help of the Holy Spirit. The Lord is our shield and buckler, our strong tower. We run to Him and are safe. I pity those who have this theology but have never experienced its reality. I pity the weakness of that Christian life because it will fall in cowardice and timidity in the face of its enemies. The slightest thing will cause the feelings to be offended. Once the feelings are offended the person sinks down into despair and self-pity because they do not know who walks along side of them! They do not know what God is offering to them in the power of the Holy Spirit.

There are many weapons Satan uses to bring discouragement - things such as sin, false accusations, relentless opposition, and disappointments. Just consider what Satan can produce by fatigue. Satan likes to get you tired and distracted. Most do not even realize how easily Satan operates on them when they are tired. Satan takes advantage of your busy schedule. You are too busy to pray, too busy to study your Bible, too busy to be at church. He sees that you are becoming fatigued and immediately works to drain and distract you from the presence of the Holy Spirit. Satan's objective is to cut you off from the provision that God alone can supply while you abide in God's presence!

Yet even when it seems the enemy has prevailed against you and all courage is gone, the Holy Spirit will not fail to love and rescue you from this plight. In a moment he can bring you out of that weakness and revitalize your relationship with the Lord.

Satan's purpose is to weaken, discourage, and destroy the child of God. The devil wants you to live in fear and despair. How frustrated he must be when someone he almost defeated is suddenly encouraged!

Remember how the Holy Spirit encouraged Joshua? The devil almost had Joshua and Israel at Moses' death. What would you have done if you had been Joshua? The greatest historical leader of all time (with the exception of Jesus Christ) has to have been Moses. He brought a nation out of four hundred years of slavery. He delivered several million people from the most powerful nation of his day. He gave them a law upon which modern nations have built their civilizations. Whenever Israel faced judgment, Moses could walk right into the presence of God and speak face to face with the Almighty like a man speaks with his friend. Moses got Israel out of trouble with the Lord! Now Joshua must take over and fill the shoes of this great man! Were it not for God giving courage, Israel would have been wiped out in the wilderness.

Israel was in despair at the death of Moses. Surely Satan must have thought that he would win the day now and prevail over this motley crew. But in that moment of despair God comes and instructs Joshua to rise and be strong and of good courage. That word from God changed the complexion of the whole situation for Israel that day. Moses had died, but the God of Israel was still alive! God transformed Joshua and put courage into His new servant to live in a way he never thought possible. God told Joshua, "... as I was with Moses so will I be with you."

BELIEVERS TAKE IT SERIOUSLY

Satan is trying to knock us out, and his ability is real. We live in a war zone. The Bible calls the last days "perilous!" "Let us hold fast the profession of *our* faith without wavering; (for he *is* faithful that promised ;) And let us consider one another to provoke unto love and to good works: Not forsaking the assembling of ourselves together, as the manner of some *is*; but exhorting *one another*: and so much the more, as ye see the day approaching" (Hebrews 10:23 – 25).

For all who are looking for a role in the body of Christ or trying to discover their gift, well here it is: "Consider one another to provoke one another unto good works ...and exhort one another ...." Rarely is a believer acting more in the Spirit than when he is found putting courage within the people of God.

If you are not involved in a church fellowship, if you are not spending time with the people of God, then you cannot consider others. You cannot consider a person unless you know that person. To consider is to know someone so well that when you are around them, you can tell if they are in need of help. You can tell by their facial expression. People that bounce around from one church to another having no place of fellowship, no intimacy with the body are in a very dangerous position.

Kent Hughes, who pastors the College Church in Wheaton, Illinois, grieves:

Church attendance is infected with a malaise of conditional loyalty which has produced an army of ecclesiastical hitch hikers. The hitch hiker's thumb says, 'You buy the car, pay for the repairs, and upkeep and insurance, fill the car with gas – and I'll ride with you. But if you have an accident, you're on your own! And I'll probably sue.' So it is with the credo of so many of today's church attenders: "You go to the meetings and serve on the boards and committees, you grapple with the issues and do the work of the church and pay the bills – I'll come along for the ride. But if things do not suit me, I'll criticize and complain, and probably bail out – my thumb is always out for a better ride. A person who lives this way does not know what he is missing. I think it is wonderful to live in the body of Christ where people know me so well that they approach me (the pastor of the church) and want to find out about my prayer life. They notice how busy things have been and want to know if I am able to continue spending time with God in prayer as I should.

But this type of accountability is rare today. Believers are so ill-established in the love of God that they grumble and complain about the slightest disturbances. Many get offended when someone expresses concern about their life. They think people are coming against them. But people are not coming against them; they are coming for them. Perhaps they are trying to get them to see things that they are not seeing clearly. They come in grace and concern. They may not appear perfectly tactful and may be somewhat clumsy, but they are coming because they love the body of Christ.

The average believer today cannot face the genuine concern and love of other believers who are seeking to protect them from the impending dangers that they see. Therefore, some leave the churches that seek the spiritual welfare of one another for a more liberal setting where they can live any way they choose and nobody cares what they do. I had rather be in a congregation of people who know me, love me, and can help me to walk and live right than to hide in a place where nobody knows me or cares to help me live righteously.

The way believers encourage is by exhorting, which means to encourage. We share the truth of God's Word. It is not our words that encourage people but the Word of God which dwells within us. For example, if someone is suffering because we have not considered them, we exhort through the Word of God about suffering. And by giving the promises of God we are able to put courage into the lives of believers and strengthen their faith.

The Bible tells us that the last days will be perilous times. We are commanded to exhort one another all the more as we see that day approaching. With all the things that believers can do and say, there is nothing more needful than for believers to help one another stay strong till the coming of Jesus Christ. Satan is trying to knock us out. We must help each other carry on. If a brother has stumbled in sin, encourage him to repent and continue in Christ. If a brother is struggling with unbelief, exhort him to believe! Our actions should not cause more despair but bring joy and hope.

It is easy to be the source of despair, but instead you can be an instrument of the Holy Spirit to build strength in believers. I am encouraged by strong preaching and truthful confrontations. I am not suggesting that we overlook sinful behavior because we don't want to offend. Sometimes it is necessary to offend the sinning believer so that he can escape a pattern of destructive behavior, and this too is exhortation. Encouragement is not overlooking a person's sin to make him feel better, but exposing that person's sin and showing the remedy in the blood of Jesus Christ!

"So comfort and encourage each other with this news..." (I Thess. 4:8).

"So encourage each other to build each other up, just as you are already doing.(I Thess. 5:11).

"Now we exhort you, brethren, warn those who are unruly, comfort [encourage] the fainthearted, uphold the weak, be patient with al ..." (I Thess. 5:14).

"But exhort [encourage] one another daily, while it is called "Today," lest any of you be hardened through the deceitfulness of sin..."(Hebrews 3:13).

God is constantly encouraging us:

I know the plans I have for you ...
I will perfect that which concerns you ...

As to sin,
As to fear,
As to rejection,
As to loss,
As to confusion,
As to hopelessness,
As to aimlessness,
As to failure.

If you have the choice to do anything, why wouldn't it be to encourage?

CHAPTER 11

SERVING THE BODY IN PRAYER

If ye abide in me, and my words abide in you, ye shall ask what ye will, and it shall be done unto you. Herein is my Father glorified, that ye bear much fruit; so shall ye be my disciples (John 15:7-8).

Perhaps nothing is more expedient within the body of Christ than the prayers believers are able to offer on behalf of others; not to mention, God is highly pleased when His children are in earnest intercession for one another. It is as if prayer were the food of God. He delights in our prayers and finds fervent prayer to be very satisfying.

Nothing will more quickly open the heavens upon a people than when those people are in earnest for one another before the throne of God. It is here, in this display of love's labor, that God is most pleased! Before the throne of God we are able to succor for our loved ones the benefits of God's assistance and outpoured benevolence. Could any act of hospitality be superior? If a man could offer the arm of the flesh to assist his fellow or could gain the omnipotence of God's arm for that friend, then you tell me which would be the higher act of hospitality?

> If ye abide in me, and my words abide in you, ye shall ask what ye will, and it shall be done unto you. Herein is my Father glorified, that ye bear much fruit; so shall ye be my disciples (John 15:7-8).

Notice that God is glorified in our fruit. There is a relationship between the fruit we bear and the prayers we pray. When God's word dwells within us, then we ask according to that word. God looks to those who believe His word. God is glorified when we come to Him believing that He will perform the Word He has spoken. God longs to be mighty for His people. God longs for a people to deliver, a people to help, to heal, to support! The evidence that we believe God's Word and that His Word abides in us is that we "ask"! Because the Word of God lives within the believer, we are encouraged to "ask what ye will." This act of faith will cause us to experience the actions of our Father in heaven. God will be glorified and the believer will be filled with joy.

These things have I spoken unto you, that my joy might remain in you, and that your joy might be full. (John 15:11).

Can you understand this great truth? God has distinguished Himself as being different from all other gods because He is the only one that can help you, and He longs for you to call on Him for that purpose!

Notice how God is glorified in the 50th Psalm:

Will I eat the flesh of bulls, or drink the blood of goats? Offer unto God thanksgiving; and pay thy vows unto the most High: And call upon me in the day of trouble: I will deliver thee, and thou shalt glorify me (Psalm 50:13-15).

Also notice why God's people are HAPPY in the 144th Psalm!

Rid me, and deliver me from the hand of strange children, whose mouth speaketh vanity, and their right hand is a right hand of falsehood: That our sons may be as plants grown up in their youth; that our daughters may be as corner stones, polished after the similitude of a palace:
That our garners may be full, affording all manner of store: that our sheep may bring forth thousands and ten thousands in our streets: That our oxen may be strong to labour; that there be no breaking in, nor going out; that there be no complaining in our streets. ***Happy is that people, that is in such a case: yea, happy is that people, whose God is the LORD*** (Psalm 144:11-15).

These people are happy because they are delivered; their children are strong; their fields are full; their cattle are healthy! And why is God glorified? Because His people are happy that their God is the Lord!

EPAPHRAS – A MODEL OF PRAYER

There is found in Colossians an obscure believer who practiced this prayerful hospitality. "Epaphras, who is one of you, a servant of Christ, saluteth you, always labouring fervently for you in prayers, that ye may stand perfect and complete in all the will of God" (Colossians 4:12).

So little is known of Epaphras, but how great is his labor: His labor was the labor of the closet, behind closed doors in the sanctuary before God. He is not mentioned as a powerful preacher, writer, or missionary – all of which are noble endeavors. He is only accredited with this one single quality; the Holy Spirit says of him, *"a man of prayer."* By this act of intercessory prayer he is a servant of Christ. His prayers went up before God that the church would stand perfect and complete in all the will of God.

We are thankful for the preachers...

The travelers ...

The writers...

But the men of prayer, who labor in their closets, are indispensable! Someone once said,

A prayerless man is a sapless man.

A prayerless preacher is a profitless preacher.

A prayerless writer will send forth barren pages.

A prayerless pastor will have little food for the flock.

If our deeds are not the fruit of spending time in the presence of God, then those deeds must be vain - the work of the flesh at best.

GOD WANTS YOU TO WALK WITH HIM, NOT SIMPLY WORK FOR HIM

It is possible to spend your life in the work of God and yet never walk with God. It is so easy to teach principles and send zealous people off to work for God – but there is a better way!

> Though I speak with the tongues of men and of angels, and have not charity, I am become as sounding brass, or a tinkling cymbal.
> And though I have the gift of prophecy, and understand all mysteries, and all knowledge; and though I have all faith, so that I could remove mountains, and have not charity, I am nothing.
> And though I bestow all my goods to feed the poor, and though I give my body to be burned, and have not charity, it profiteth me nothing.
> Charity suffereth long, and is kind; charity envieth not; charity vaunteth not itself, is not puffed up, Doth not behave itself unseemly, seeketh not her own, is not easily provoked, thinketh no evil; Rejoiceth not in iniquity, but rejoiceth in the truth; Beareth all things, believeth all things, hopeth all things, endureth all things.   Charity never faileth... (1 Corinthians 13:1-8).

THE SHOW OF TRUE LOVE IS PRAYER

Many judge others as lacking compassion because of their physical absence in a time of crisis, rarely considering their spiritual labor before the throne of God. Again, if a man could offer the arm of the flesh to assist his fellow, or he could gain the omnipotence of God's arm for that friend; then you tell me which would be the higher act of hospitality? If, instead of gaining your attention, he were to flee alone before the throne of God to succor for you the benefits of God's assistance and outpoured benevolence, would that not be the greatest labor a human could give you?

If all Epaphras did was to carry out that hidden labor before the throne of God, then it is possible that many would consider him deficient in his zeal for the things of God. And he would be judged thus simply because he was not visibly present before the people! Because many will look with a carnal mind, rather than a spiritual mind, they will judge Epaphras as deficient because they see no outward physical work. But the Holy Ghost lifts him up as a man greatly affecting the cause of Christ.

It is a false standard simply to measure a man's care or sympathy by his visits or letters. You have no idea how many times God has brought you through because of the praying friend, pastor, or church!

Love is displayed by the fervent prayers that are offered on behalf of others!

> A love of writing may lead me to write ...
> > A love of travel may cause me to go ...
> > > A love of preaching may make me preach ...
> > > > A love of self may cause me to make myself necessary to you ...

But nothing but a love for souls, a love for Christ, could ever cause me to agonize on your behalf, or to seek His mind to feed you as His flock, "...that you may stand perfect and complete in all the will of God." Are you praying for those you love? Are you praying for the church you belong to? Are you praying for the church's young people?

A card in the mail reads,

> We are teenagers. We are the first generation to grow up with Point-and-click Pornography. Almost all of us (90%) have viewed porn online ... most while doing homework. In fact we view more internet Porn than any other age group. But that shouldn't shock you. Not when you consider that we see nearly 14,000 sexual scenes and references each year on television. That's more than 38 a day.

Another reads,

> We are teenagers. The new generation. We may look OK at
> first Glance, but we are not well. One million of us are preg-
> nant. 750 of us get ABORTIONS each year! Forty-percent of
> us have purposefully cut ourselves…because we hurt so bad
> on the inside. And more than 1500 of us will take our own
> lives this year.

I AM NOT REFERRING SIMPLY TO SAYING PRAYERS

Now I am not referring to the ritual act of simply saying prayers.
I am talking about labor - a spiritual vigor that actually accomplishes
much for the people of God! I am referring to those who pray "…
according TO THE POWER that works in them …."

> Now unto him that is able to do exceeding abundantly above
> all that we ask or think, according to the power that worketh
> in us … (Ephesians 3:20).

This is something grand, beyond our thoughts and comprehension:

> It is the hope of life …
> > The hope of society …
> > > The grand purpose …
> > > > The absolute victory …

> Likewise the Spirit also helpeth our infirmities: for we know
> not what we should pray for as we ought: but the Spirit itself
> maketh intercession for us with groanings which cannot be
> uttered. And he that searcheth the hearts knoweth what is the
> mind of the Spirit, because he maketh intercession for the
> saints according to the will of God (Romans 8:26-27).

Look at Hannah! She prayed life where there was death: "…I *am*
a woman of a sorrowful spirit … [and] have poured out my soul
before the LORD" (1 Samuel 1:15*)*.

Her prayer is answered and her reproach is removed. Who can remember the names of Peninnah's children? But God gave Hannah more than she thought or asked! Samuel was born of a praying mother and he was a praying man – God knew him. God was affected by his prayers!

Jean-Nicolas Grou prayed,

O my Savior, I say to Thee again with more insistence than ever: Teach me to pray; implant in me all the dispositions needful for the prayer of the Holy Spirit to make me humble, simple, and docile; may I do all that is in my power to become... what use is my prayer if the Holy Spirit does not pray with me? Come, Holy Spirit come to dwell and work within me! Take possession of my understanding and of my will; govern my actions not only at the moment of prayer but at every moment. I cannot glorify God nor sanctify myself save by Thee.

God has never worked alongside the prayerless man or counted on him for eternal things.

It was a praying Jonah who went to Nineveh! True prayer is not me taking hold of God but God taking hold of me, just like God took hold of Nehemiah and Daniel.

In the afternoon 'God was with me of a truth.' Oh, it was blessed company indeed! God enabled me so to agonize in prayer that I was quite wet with sweat, though in the shade and the cool wind. My soul was drawn out very much for the world; I grasped for multitudes of souls. I think I had more enlargement for sinners than for the children of God, though I felt as if I could spend my life in cries for both. I enjoyed great sweetness in communion with my dear Saviour. I think I never in my life felt such an entire weanedness from this world and so much resigned to God in everything. Oh, that I may always live to God!

- David Brainerd (1740)

If that power is not yours, if that promise is not your possession, then so be it. But if you claim that Jesus is speaking to you in John 15 and Ephesians 3 then this is your moment – "He is able to do ... according to the power that worketh in us." Don't you sit back thinking, "Well Jesus is coming soon anyway!" You do not have that luxury – you will answer to that King for how His kingdom faired in your day!

"God is able..." Jesus said, "Nothing shall be impossible to you ..." Things may appear impossible. There will be a struggle. But nothing is impossible when the Holy Spirit can pray through you.

Leonard Ravenhill said,

> Every church without a prayer meeting condemns us; every Bible daily unopened condemns us; every promise of God unused condemns us; every unreached neighbor condemns us; every dry eye among us condemns us; every wasted minute of our time condemns us; every unclaimed opportunity for God condemns us. Next year is not ours. Tomorrow may be too late. Unless we repent now, unless we return and fire the prayer altars now, unless we fast and weep now, woe unto us at the judgment!

CONTACT INFORMATION:

Pastor Lee Shipp may be reached for ministry by contacting:

First New Testament Church
3235 Aubin Lane
Baton Rouge, La. 70816
USA

(225) 293-2222

Pastor Shipp's Email address is:
Office@fntchurch.org
ctoh@fntchurch.org

Please visit us at: www.fntchurch.org

ABOUT THE AUTHOR

P astor Lee Shipp, as the founder and senior pastor of First New Testament Church, has ministered God's Word through the power of the Holy Spirit for over twenty-five years. Led by a devotion to his Savior and a love for the scriptures, God has used him to teach and preach throughout the world, through conferences, camp meetings, and revivals. Pastor Shipp is also founder and President of "A Call to the Heart"; a ministry of evangelism and outreach through radio, T.V., literature, and national and international campaigns. As well, Pastor Shipp also serves on the Board of Directors for "The School of Christ International." Pastor Shipp and his family live in Baton Rouge, Louisiana where they continue to serve the Lord with their church family.

www.fntchurch.org

Parents will sleep in the hospital waiting room tonight. A husband will sleep on a couch in a critical care unit crying to a God he probably does not know! Where is the church in this hour?

What does God think when we pray, "God what is your will for my life? What would you have me to do?"

He would say, "Take my Love to the streets. Walk through a hospital waiting room, serve and minister to the scared and hurting! Relieve the wife who is strangled with fear. Undo the burdens of the man who just got laid off from his job. Take my lovingkindness to the schools and offer the teenage girl, starving for affection, my love. Go into the places where people are hurting. If they will not let you in, then find the places that will."

By human measurements, religion has set standards regarding spiritual status and significance which most people sitting in our congregations will never attain. One of those measurements is that a Man of God must be in full-time ministry, such as a pastor or evangelist. Such a standard is disastrous and discouraging because most believers will never be called to an office in the Body of Christ.

Most Christians will live their entire lives having never raised the dead. Most will never walk on water. Most will never speak to a large crowd of people. Most will never see thousands of people come to Christ as a result of their preaching ministry. However, anybody can do the things that please God: Feeding the hungry, clothing the naked, ministering to the needy, and preaching the gospel to the poor. What an impact. You don't need the elaborate, you need the common.

CPSIA information can be obtained at www.ICGtesting.com
Printed in the USA
LVOW102003190312

273728LV00001B/4/P